101 Tips for Families With Teens

Staying A Step Ahead

Megan Egerton
&
John Willman

Please Read

The authors have done their best to present accurate and up-to-date information in this book, but they cannot guarantee that the information is correct or will suit your particular situation. This book is sold with the understanding that the publisher and authors are not engaged in rendering legal, accounting, counselling or any other professional services. If expert assistance is required, the services of a competent professional should be sought.

Copyright 2011 Egerton Graham Consulting
ISBN 978-0-9868724-0-2
Version 1.1

Author: Megan Egerton Graham

Design and Illustration: John Willman

Published by Egerton Graham Consulting
www.egertongrahamcons

For my parents who let me survive my own teen years. Without their patience, unconditional love and support I wouldn't have survived my own teen years!

Forward

This book is intended to support families with tweens and teens. When it comes to your children, I believe that the more information you have, the better and easier your decision making process will be. Tweens and teens work hard to keep you guessing; this book gives you quick, easy to read tips on how to worm your way into their lives, keep them safe and happy(ier) as they grow up, change schools, meet and loose friends, or just being a teen in a modern household.

Ask Questions

"Families are about love and overcoming emotional torture."

— *Matt Groening*

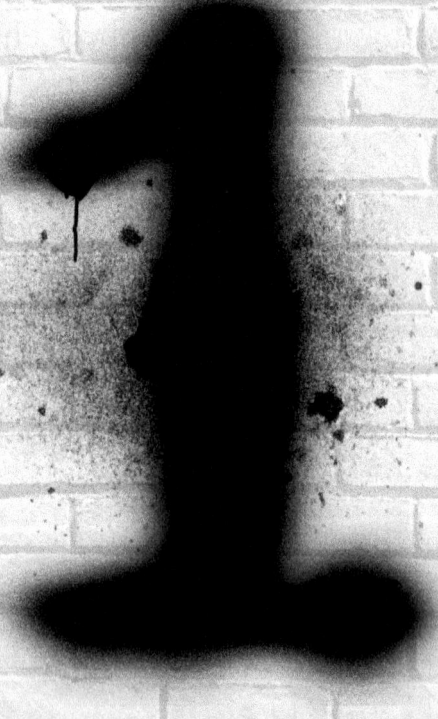

With teens, if you don't ask you definitely won't find out. Ask questions every day in different ways; don't get discouraged if all you get is a grunt. Asking questions shows you care and are interested. Be prepared to hear some answers you may not like.

Suggestions

- Ask the same question more than once and in different ways
- Try not to react negatively if it is not the answer you were hoping for
- Show a genuine interest in getting an answer and actively listen (turn off radio, TV, or other distraction)
- If you aren't sure what they mean ask them a probing question (when you say _____, do you mean that you _____?)
- Don't let silence intimidate you; give them enough time to answer the questions you ask before asking others

Be Honest

"It takes two to share the truth — one to speak, and another to hear."

—Henry David Thoreau

We ask teenagers to be open and honest with their parents and yet it is not always reciprocated! Be honest when asked difficult questions answer them with the same openness and honesty you are expecting from them. Teenagers can sense and smell dishonesty from a mile off!

Suggestions

- It is actually good to admit you don't have all the answers – if you don't know, say so
- If they ask you questions, take time to answer them truthfully and as accurately as possible
- When asked for honesty try to stick to facts more than opinions – at this point in their lives your opinion is somewhat valued but facts are much more important
- Don't confuse criticism with honesty

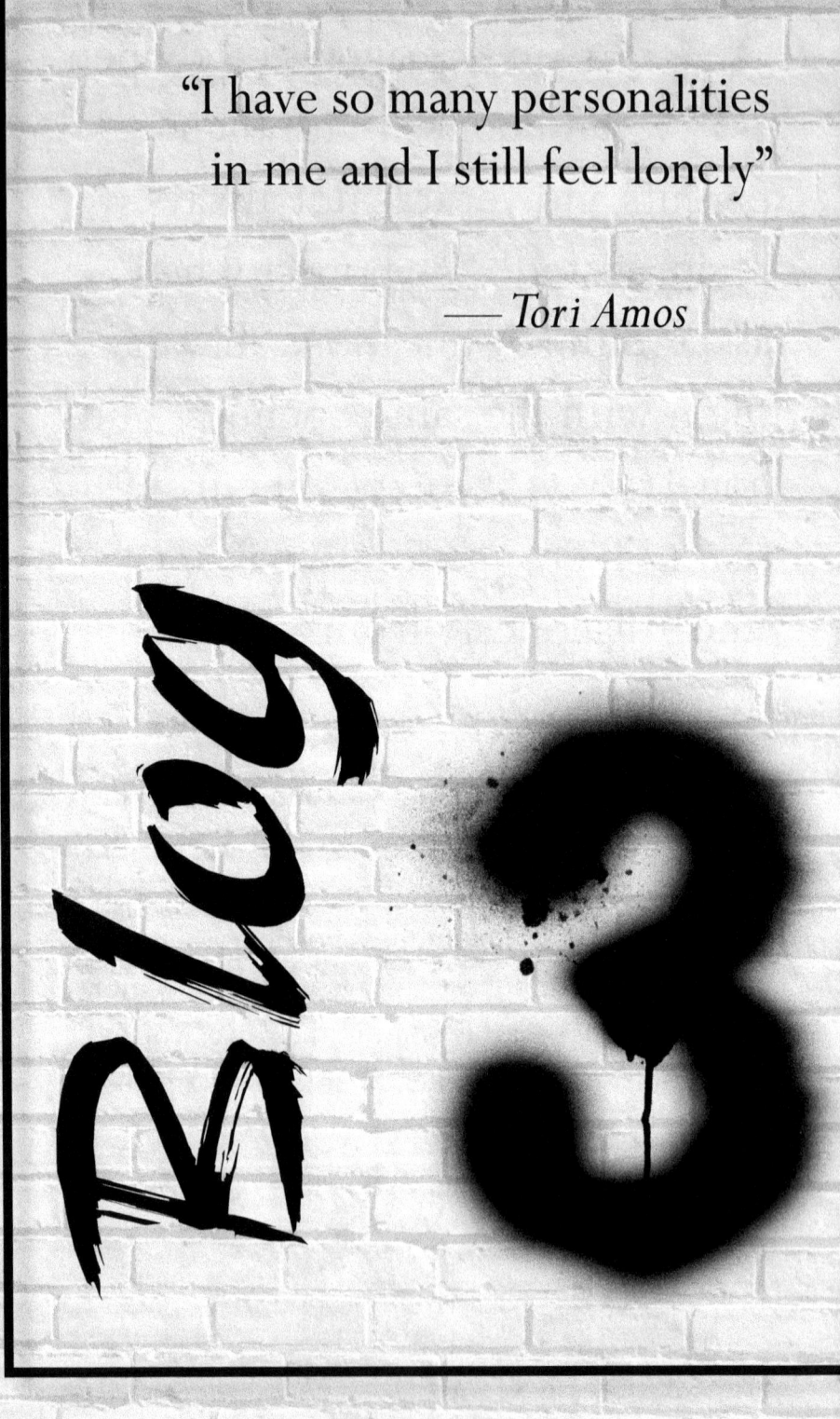

"I have so many personalities in me and I still feel lonely"

— *Tori Amos*

Blog 3

Let them purge their angst! Blogs help them process their feelings and keep a daily accounting of their lives, what is important to them, their dreams, goals and ambitions; it is another method of improving their writing and communication skills.

Suggestions

- Put them in charge of a family blog so that an family members who may be miles away can catch up on daily or weekly 'happenings' in your household just by logging on — anywhere in the world
- Remind them that anyone can access it and not to write detailed, identifying information or anything that they would not want other people to read
- Make it part of their routine or the family routine
- Don't let it become another stress or burden — let them dictate when they will write

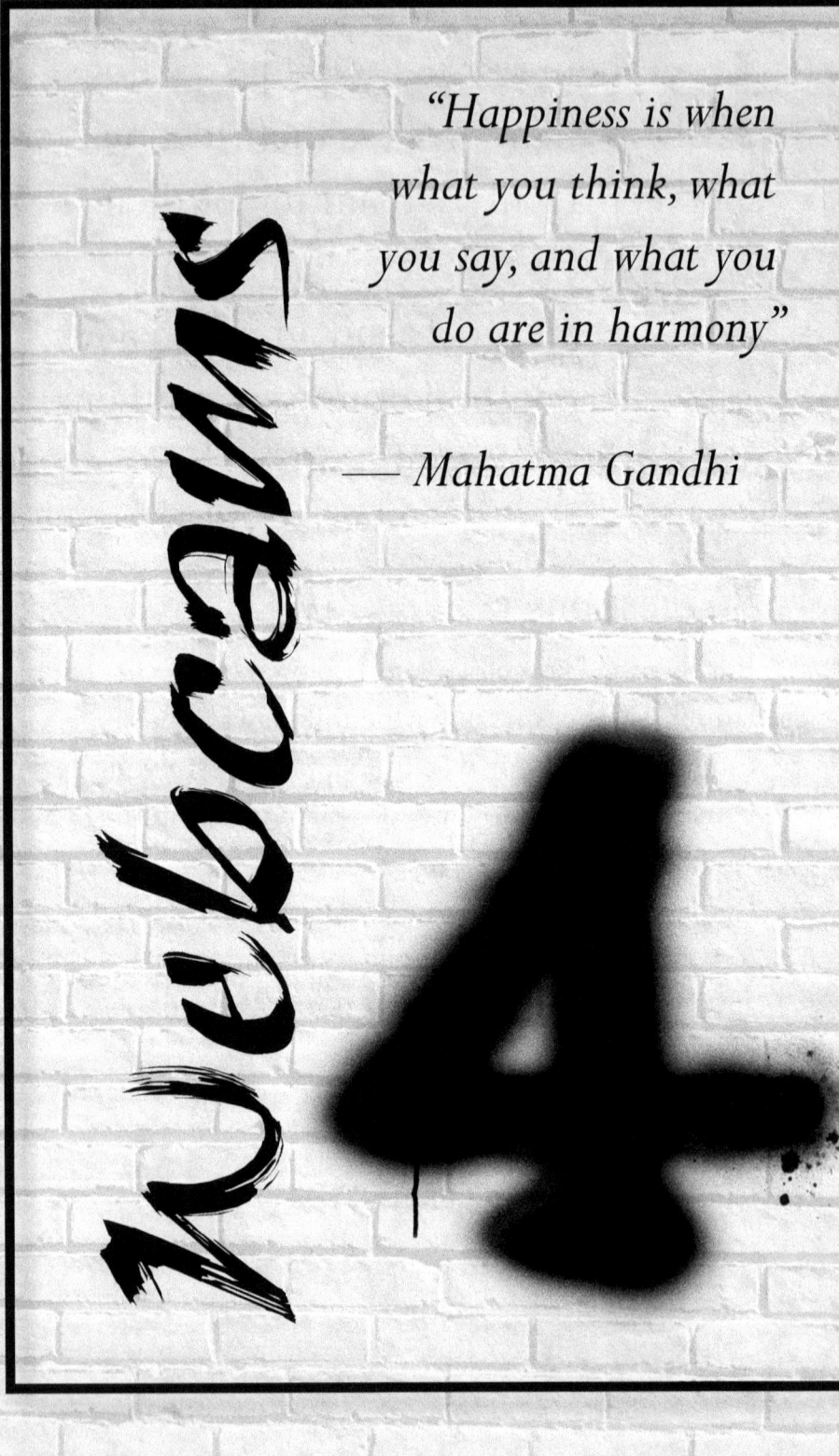

Webcams can be a great way to not only talk to friends but family too. A lot of comfort can be drawn from seeing friendly face and a smile. Sometimes they need to connect to someone that isn't immediate family but also loves and understands their family dynamic.

Suggestions

- Make sure that the webcam is in a central location in your home where it is easily visible and in a high traffic area
- Set up times when the entire family to get together and talk to family members or friends so everyone is aware of how it works and knows how to use it.
- If you have several people in your family and limited time, put a timer by the computer so that everyone has equal time to go on
- If you want to reduce delays, use the webcam so that you can see each other and a separate phone line (cell or home phone) so that you can get better voice quality and in real time

Write Letters

> "Intellectuals solve problems, geniuses prevent them"
>
> — Albert Einstein

5

Write to your teen. Sometimes just saying something isn't enough they need to know you mean it. In the letter list all of the things that you love, admire and respect about that person. Committing important sentiments to paper helps us to really believe in it and makes sure that significant things are not left unsaid.

Suggestions

- Talk about special qualities and brainstorm together about things you could write to each other to get everyone thinking
- Get special paper and envelopes to use
- Don't write letters that are done under pressure or rushed
- Make sure that you put the letter in a private spot where other friends or family won't come across it and put your teen on the spot

Ready 6

> "Material possessions rust away, wear away or depreciate. Character alone will never tarnish"
>
> — Elizabeth Dole

Teens need a break from their reality. Losing themselves in a book or magazine is a healthy escape from their daily lives and can reduce stress and anxiety. A lot of what we learn about ourselves comes from the things we read. Teens identify who they are as people through comparing themselves with others – both real and fictional.

Suggestions

- Get a variety of books and magazines and leave them in different areas of the house
- Check to see if the content is appropriate. Read the first, middle and last pages of the book - if you have time, read the whole thing
- Read the same book and then you have something to talk about
- Model reading as a way of taking time for yourself – if you read, they will too (eventually)
- Go on www.wywa.org and see our recommended teen books
- Depending on what is happening in their worlds – choose books carefully

Organize

> "Life is too complicated not to be orderly"
>
> — Martha Stewart

7

Keeping yourself and your teen organized is essential to their survival and yours! Their minds are disorganized at the best of times and if you then create a disorganized environment you are asking for trouble.

Suggestions

- Keep yourself organized with a simple system. If you aren't organized, they won't be.
- Let everyone know what the systems in the house are and your expectations
- Ask for input – you can be assured that they will have an opinion
- Clean out rooms every 6 months
- If it hasn't been used in 2 years, it isn't going to be.
- Set aside time weekly to sort piles, laundry, desk tops, etc.
- Pay them to do it – money talks and being organized is a critical component to being successful academically and socially

Act, don't react

> "Some people say you are going the wrong way, when it's simply a way of your own"
>
> —Angelina Jolie

8

We are human and sometimes the things that come out of teenagers mouths naturally cause us to have adverse reactions. Many times they are looking for a reaction. Think before responding and take the time to think about what actions should be taken, rather than going with your first reaction.

Suggestions

- React immediately only in emergencies
- Listen to what they have said and then ask yourself what their intentions might be
- Ask them questions to clarify, before responding – it will buy you time
- Ask them how they think you should respond
- Remember not to always respond with their timelines in mind (they often feel things are urgent when there are days/weeks/months before a decision needs to be made)
- Give yourself a time out if you are angry, call a friend/family member, etc.

set boundaries

"Everything has its limit — iron ore cannot be educated into gold"

— *Mark Twain*

You have limits and they should know what they are. Think of your boundaries much like a high cement wall – not easy to climb, move or breakdown! Your family needs to know where you stand on important issues.

Suggestions

- Take time each day to talk about 'what ifs' – how they would react and how you would react, etc.
- Buy "If" books or " go to ww.wywa.org if you need questions or scenarios
- Ask them about their friends and what they are doing, and what their limits are with their parents
- Explain your boundaries once. Do not go over it again and again. Let your teen(s) know your reasons but do not fall into the trap of having to justify yourself constantly

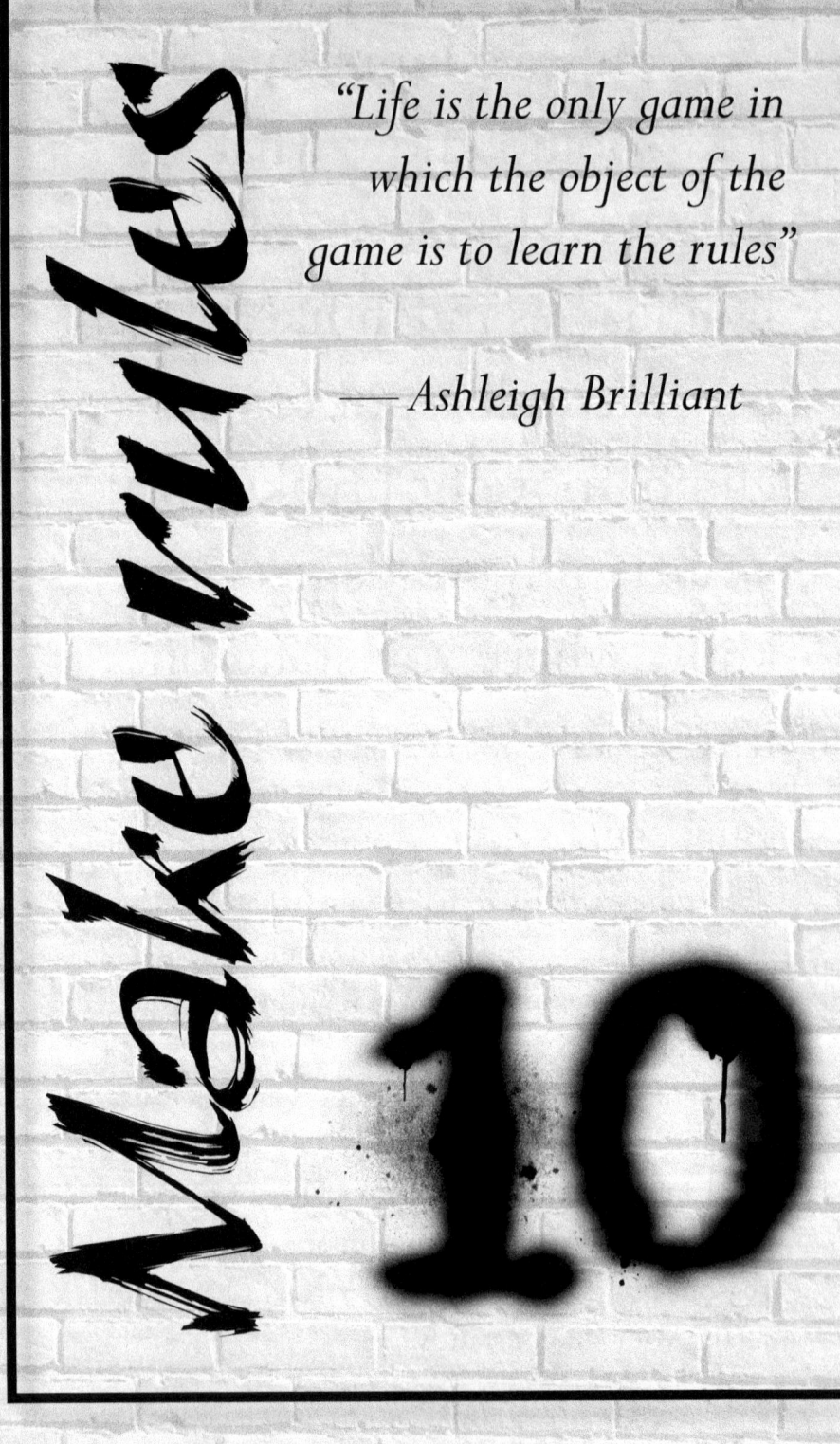

Make rules

> "Life is the only game in which the object of the game is to learn the rules"
>
> — Ashleigh Brilliant

10

Don't let your house be the only place where there aren't clear rules. We have rules for everything (how to behave at school, driving, behaviour in the workplace, socializing with people, etc.). Teens need to know what the rules are but live by them. Rules bring structure and sanity!

Suggestions
- Create rules together
- Your kids should know the consequences of their actions beforehand (you break curfew, your curfew will be even earlier; not doing chores means no allowance, etc.)
- Limit the number of house rules to a maximum of 5 (i.e., be respectful, be responsible for _____, be home by _____, complete all school work assigned, etc.)
- Let your teen(s) make a rule or two for you to follow as well
- Be ready to reinforce what you have laid out; no child will follow the rules knowing there isn't any follow through
- Reward and praise when rules are followed

know their school(s)

> "Education is the key to unlock the golden door of freedom."
>
> — George Washington Carver

11

Many parents believe that as their children get older they should gradually step back from being involved in their schooling. Junior High and High School is the time when you should be in the school, know it well and be known. The more a parent is involved the less they will be able to 'pull the wool over your eyes'.

Suggestions

- Volunteer at the school or join school/parent council
- Get the email or contact information for each of your children's teachers and introduce yourself
- Walk around the school and the area to find out what is in the immediate vicinity (local mall, store, park, etc.) that might 'distract' your child
- Go on the website to find out about staff, activities, schedules, etc.
- Make a copy of your child(ren)'s schedules and put it on the pantry or fridge door
- Attend many school sponsored events. Drag your child with you if you can, as the best communication happens when teacher, student and parent are together

> "With realization of one's own potential and self-confidence in one's ability, one can build a better world."
>
> — *Dalai Lama*

These, sometimes, dreaded papers come a few times a year and say more about your child's progress than simply marks. Look for any personal remarks that say what kind of student his/her teachers perceive them to be and try to place importance on this as often as possible. After all, we want our children to be well adjusted and happy – some accomplish this with C's and D's and some with A's and B's.

Suggestions

- Say something about the comments before the marks - whether or not the marks are A's or not
- Know the dates for when reports are sent home
- Create a file for all report cards and school documentation
- Go back and compare reports to look at improvements or areas that have declined
- Have your child set goals (maximum of three) after each report card, have them commit them to paper and sign it – it should be posted or easy to access so you can refer to those goals
- Call the school with concerns and get first hand information

Make time

"The future is something which everyone reaches at the rate of 60 minutes an hour, whatever he does, whoever he is."

— C.S. Lewis

13

Life can be busy at the best of times but making time to talk to your child (even if they appear alien-like) can save you a lot of grief later on. Think of this time as important as eating, brushing your teeth or even breathing. By making time for your teen(s) you are showing them that they are a priority and teaching them about making time for what is most important - family.

Suggestions
- Put talking to them into your daily routine
- Make a commitment to touch base for 15minutes a day per child
- If they tell you they want to talk – celebrate, and then stop what you are doing immediately and really listen to what they are saying
- Sit and watch a show with them, even if you would rather watch paint dry
- Go and watch them in a game, activity or event
- Be the parent that volunteers to drive people – a lot of good information (you may never otherwise receive) comes out of car rides with blabber-mouthed friends

keep promises

> "Keep every promise you make; only make promises you can keep."
>
> — Anthony Hitt

14

We expect our children to keep the promises they make and the best way to teach this is through modelling it ourselves. If you know you can't do something, be honest. When you make a commitment, the only things that should stop you are actual life and death emergencies, as everything else can wait.

Suggestions

- When your teen asks you to make a commitment, think about your week, month or schedule before saying yes
- Find out how important it is to your child by asking them directly rather than by your own criteria of what's important
- Use your cell phone alarm, fridge door, etc. to remind yourself of important promises
- Remind other people of what is important to you so that when you have to leave a meeting, work or some other engagement they will be more understanding (ex. "Sorry, family first" or "I am honouring my commitments to my family")
- A good motto to live by for promises is 'say what you mean and mean what you say.

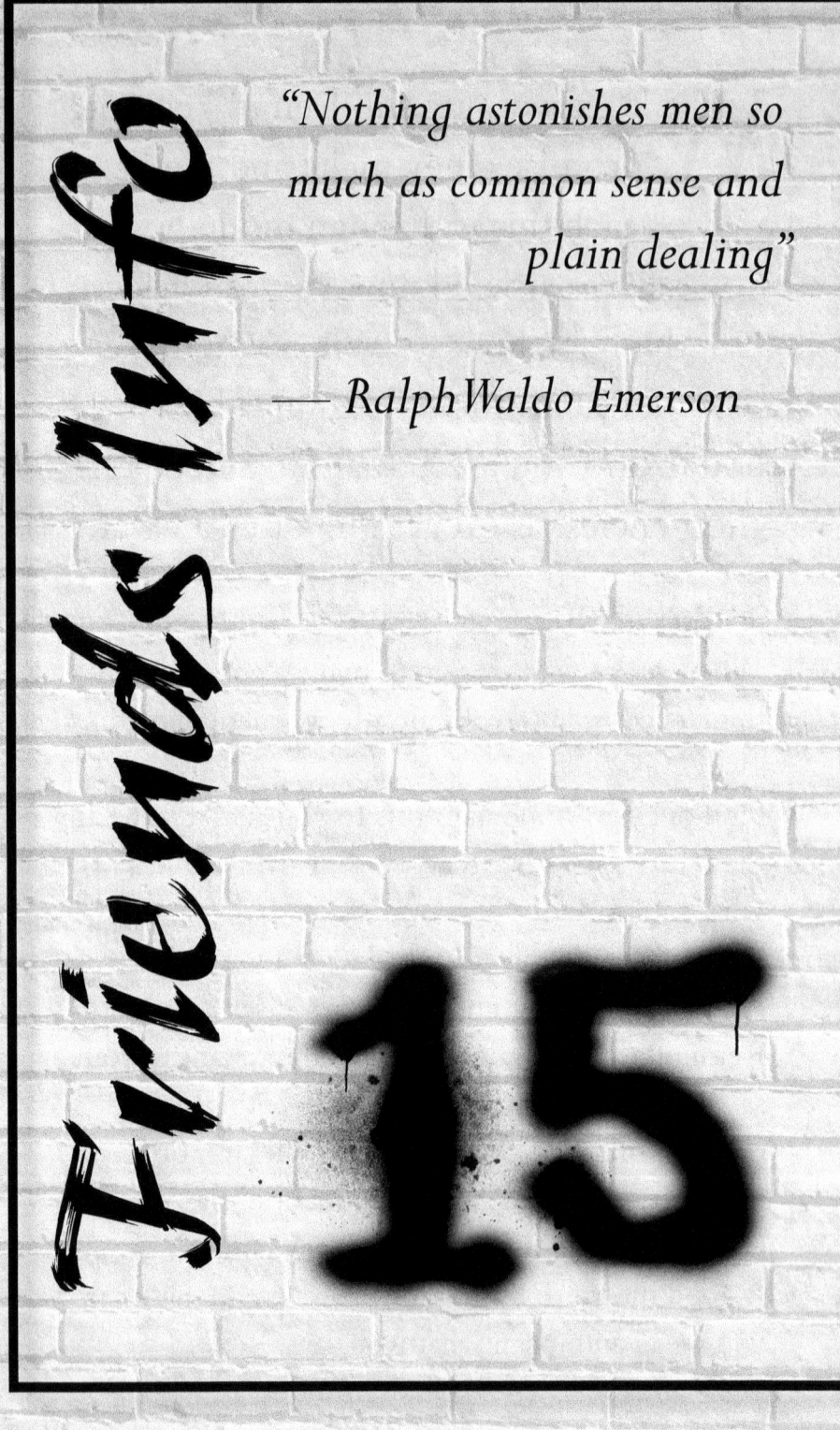

Get their friend's contact information (email addresses, cell phone numbers, addresses). Having this information will make your life less stressful when (please note – not "if" but "when") you have to hunt them down! Teen life means making new and different friends several times over and it is important to make sure that you know as much as possible about each friend.

Suggestions

- If you don't have the friend's contact information then they don't get to spend time with them
- Keep a list on the fridge or in an easy to access area
- Store as much information as you can in your personal cell phone or PDA so that it is with you at all times
- Test the information you have; if they are standing there and give you their friend's cell phone number, call it on the spot and make sure it is the actual number
- Explain your intentions and point out that it isn't to embarrass them unnecessarily

Emergency kits

16

> *"Fortune favors the prepared mind."*
>
> — Louis Pasteur

Make kits together for emergencies. Have everyone contribute and know where they are so that when you are in the middle of an emergency no one person will take the blame for not having the one useful item you actually needed. When everyone does them then everyone is aware that they exist and where to locate them when they are really needed.

Suggestions

- Candles
- Pack of cards or travel board games
- Matches and/or lighter
- Flash lights
- Batteries – assorted sizes
- Energy bars and long life food
- Bottled water
- Canned food and can opener
- Solar or wind-up radio
- Go to the American or Canadian Red Cross website for more emergency kits information
- Go through and update your kit every 6 months

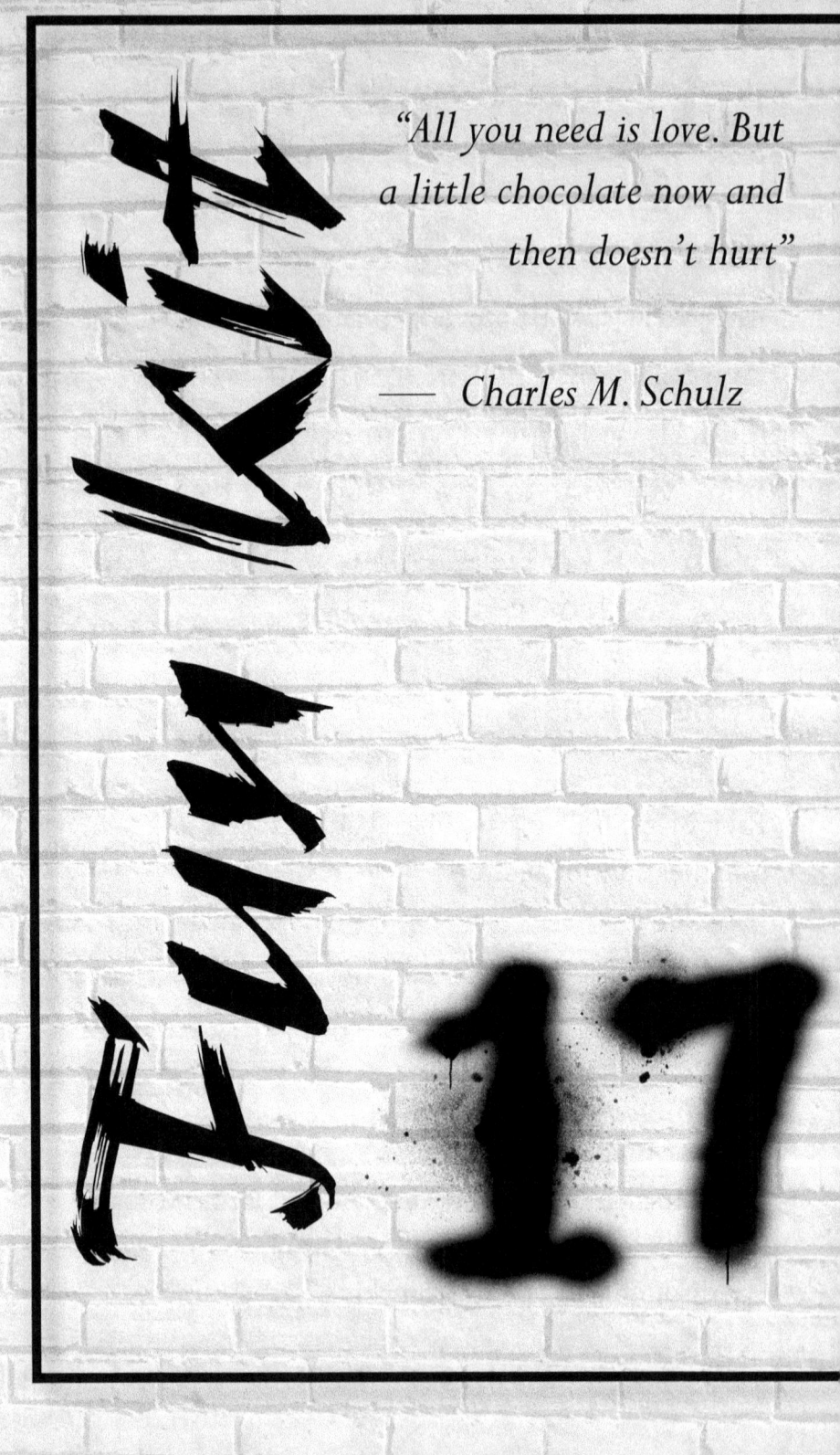

> "All you need is love. But a little chocolate now and then doesn't hurt"
>
> — Charles M. Schulz

Fun Unit 17

This kit is for those times when deep down you still all love each other but… you can't stand the sight of each other or are feeling as though another moment of whining/ complaining/ demanding will destroy you. This kit should be designed to lighten the mood, remind you all of happier moments.

Suggestions

- Food – non-perishable, junky and fun
- Favourite DVDs
- Gift certificates for favourite store(s)
- Funny pictures of family members or friends, happier times, etc.
- Some book that is loved, silly or thoughtful
- Soft new pyjamas or something comforting
- Something to pamper themselves with (nail polish, face mask, hair gel, new boxers, etc.)
- A board game to play together

Video Diary

> "I wake up laughing. Yes, I wake up in the morning and there I am just laughing my head off."
>
> — Bruce Willis

18

Keeping a video diary is an unique way of keeping track of the big and small changes and events that take place in your daily lives. It is another creative outlet for teens to experss their feelings in a personal way. It is a way of being able to actually see the changes in yourself and your family.

Suggestions

- Have several people in your family know how to operate the camera and how to transfer the information so that it is not one person's burden
- Don't say or put anything on the video that you wouldn't want other people to see or hear
- Give your children the opportunity to film privately and make an agreement ahead of time about who will hear and see the video
- Do not secretly film anyone as they may end up being resentful and refuse to participate further
- Remind everyone about expressing both positive and negative sentiments

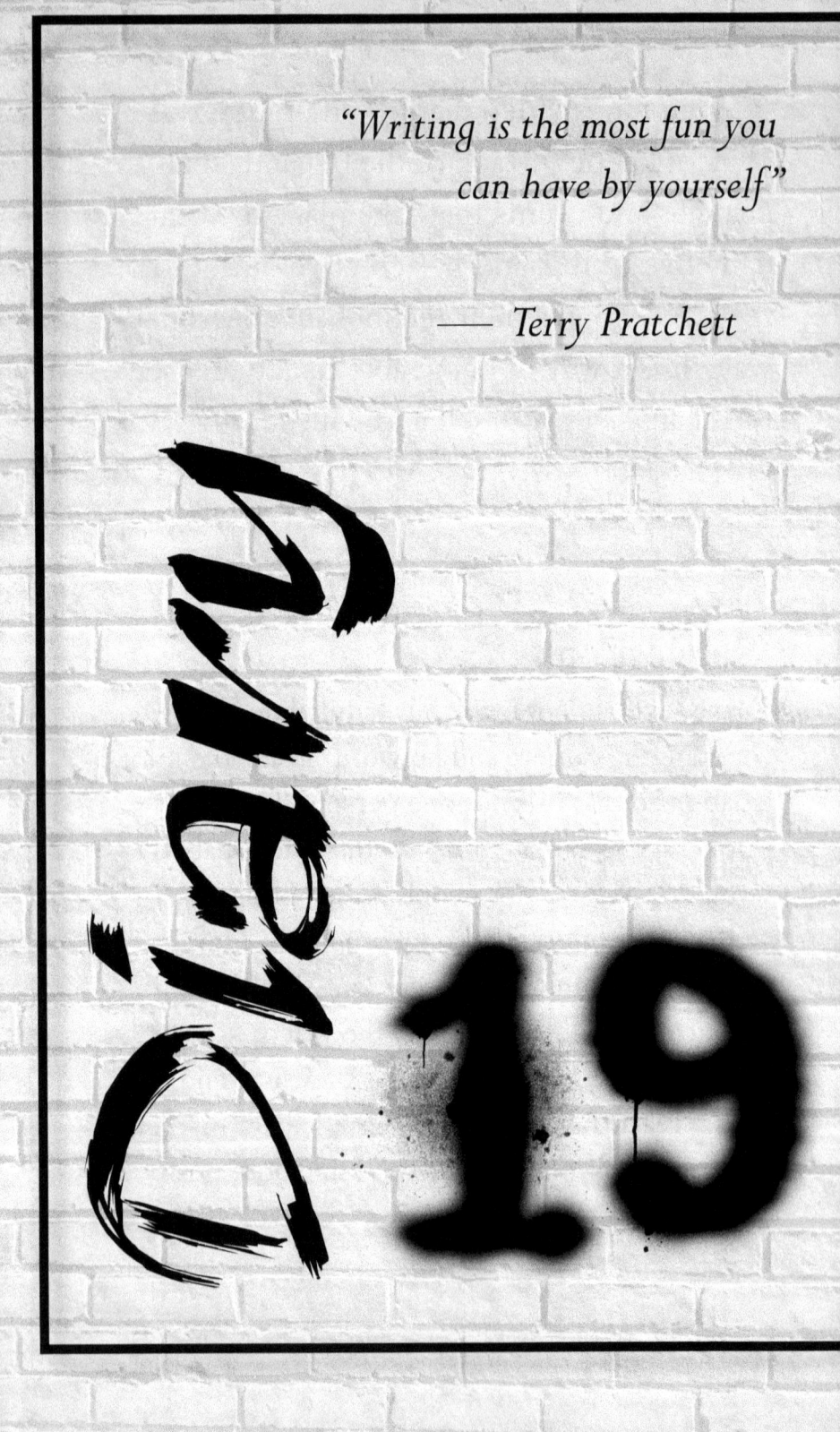

If your child chooses to write, respect their privacy and avoid any opportunity or temptations to read it. Writing down thoughts and feelings, annoyances, dreams, goals, ambitions or just organizing thoughts onto paper can be therapeutic. By committing ideas to paper they can learn to self-reflect, analyze their decisions and consider their possibilities.

Suggestions

- Let your teens know where you stand about their privacy and leaving out their diary
- Buy a fancy looking book or something with a cover that will attract them
- Use journals with topics or prompts to help them organize their thoughts (www.wywa.org)
- Don't make this a forced activity, just gently encourage it
- Model this thinking and writing process for them keeping a journal yourself and making time to regularly write in it.

"Money is not the only answer,
but it makes a difference"

— Barack Obama

Money

20

Money talks to tweens and teens and shouldn't be used to reinforce expected, basic and human decencies. BUT it can be a good motivational tool. Asking yourself "what is this worth to me?" can avoid a lot of unnecessary battling.

Suggestions

- Decide in your own mind what you are willing to pay for, and what your expectations are for feeding them, clothing them and loving them
- Look at your finances and talk about what is possible and what is not
- Do not negotiate amount. Make an offer and they can take it or leave it. If they smell weakness or doubt you will end up blowing your budget (they can't smell the rotting food or dirty socks under their beds but they can smell indecision and weakness from a mile off)
- Then create a chart that has payments and penalties. When they don't do it, fine them! ($2 to bring home agenda and homework, $2 for not doing it or $1 to set the table, $2 for not doing it and stressing me out)

Simplify

21

> "I don't know the key to success, but the key to failure is trying to please everybody."
>
> — *Bill Cosby*

Life is not simple or easy when you are a teen or tween and it is important that you take the time to make sure that your life is not filled with unimportant or unnecessary obligations and/or complications. Simplying things for yourself will naturally filter down to your children.

Suggestions

- If you always cook a huge meal on Sunday, order out sometimes instead
- Sort out closets and areas of clutter and get rid of things you haven't used in 2 years
- If your children have several different sports teams or events, see if you can get them into a car pool and do it once a month instead of once a week
- If you enjoy reading a magazine but don't like the hassle of getting it – order it online or have it delivered
- When buying food, look at the preparation methods to make sure you aren't buying a meal that will take all night
- Buy in bulk and make fewer trips to the store

set goals

> "Start wide, expand further, and never look back"
>
> — Arnold Schwarzenegger

22

Your children need to have goals for their immediate and distant future to give them a sense of hope. Encourage them to talk about their wants, dreams, ambitions and make realistic goals for themselves. Set goals for your family and model this behaviour so that they can see goals evolve, be accomplished or change as need be.

Suggestions

- Talk to your family about your personal goals – goals you have reached, have failed to accomplish, are still working on
- Ask them about their hopes and dreams and help them to identify things they could do to achieve their goals
- Make sure you steer them towards having a balance of short term goals and long term goals as they will need to feel success along the way
- Short term goals – Run a mile without stopping, lose 2Lbs, read an entire book, study for a test, be on time for curfew, etc.
- Long term goals – run a half marathon, go to university or college, get a scholarship, get married, travel the world, get high paying job, become a _____, work for _____, etc.

Pampered 23

> "To be loved, you have to be nice to others every day! To be hated, you don't have to do squat!"
>
> — *Homer Simpson*

Take time as a family to pamper yourselves and each other. Doing small yet thoughtful things for each other can often prevent blow-ups and misunderstandings. It is important to take time to spoil yourself and those around you everyone now and again. It is just another way to say "I value and love you".

Suggestions

- Get your nails, hair or toes done
- Have a fancy dinner at home or get take out
- Hire someone to cut the lawn or shovel the driveway to give someone else a break
- Pick them up from school early and go shopping for a special treat
- Buy a fancy dessert and surprise everyone with it
- Clean their room for them or do their laundry
- Get a cleaning service in
- Get tickets for a concert or show
- Leave the dishes in the sink and do them later

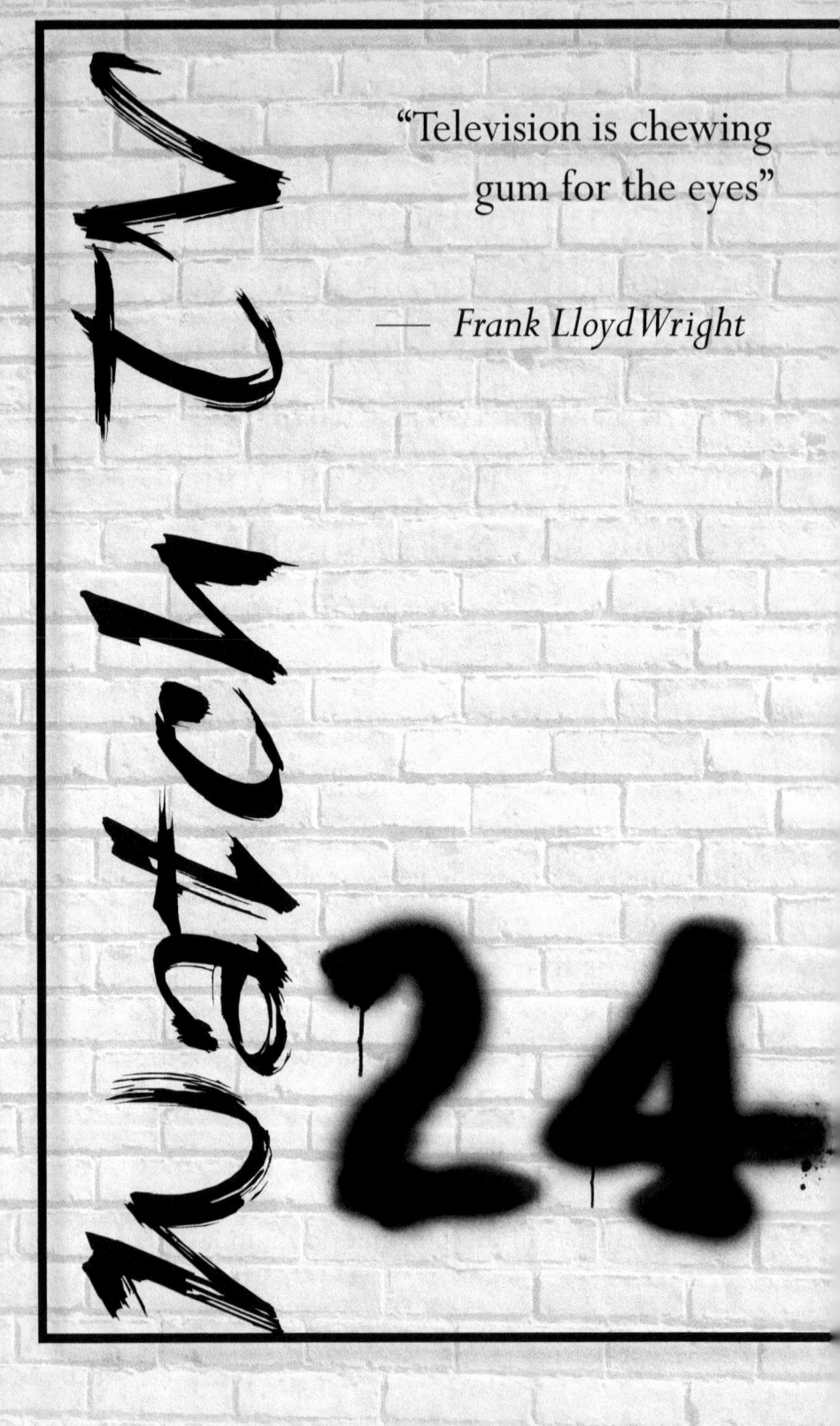

A good way to find out about how their lives are going or what their interests are is to sit and watch TV with them. The show may sicken, offend or outrage you but this is what they want to see and this is what influences them. Ask them questions about the show, their opinions about the people they are watching and take a genuine interest in what entertains them.

Suggestions

- Don't ask too many questions all at once
- Wait for commercials or opportune times to ask questions
- Do not be judgemental or offer too many of your own opinions (unless asked)
- Don't be afraid to ask why they are watching this type of show
- Pick something positive to say about it, dig deep and find a redeeming quality to focus on
- Have your TV in a central location in the house
- Avoid having a TV in their bedrooms (you don't know what they are watching, how late they are watching and it will reduce opportunities to communicate or spend time with them)

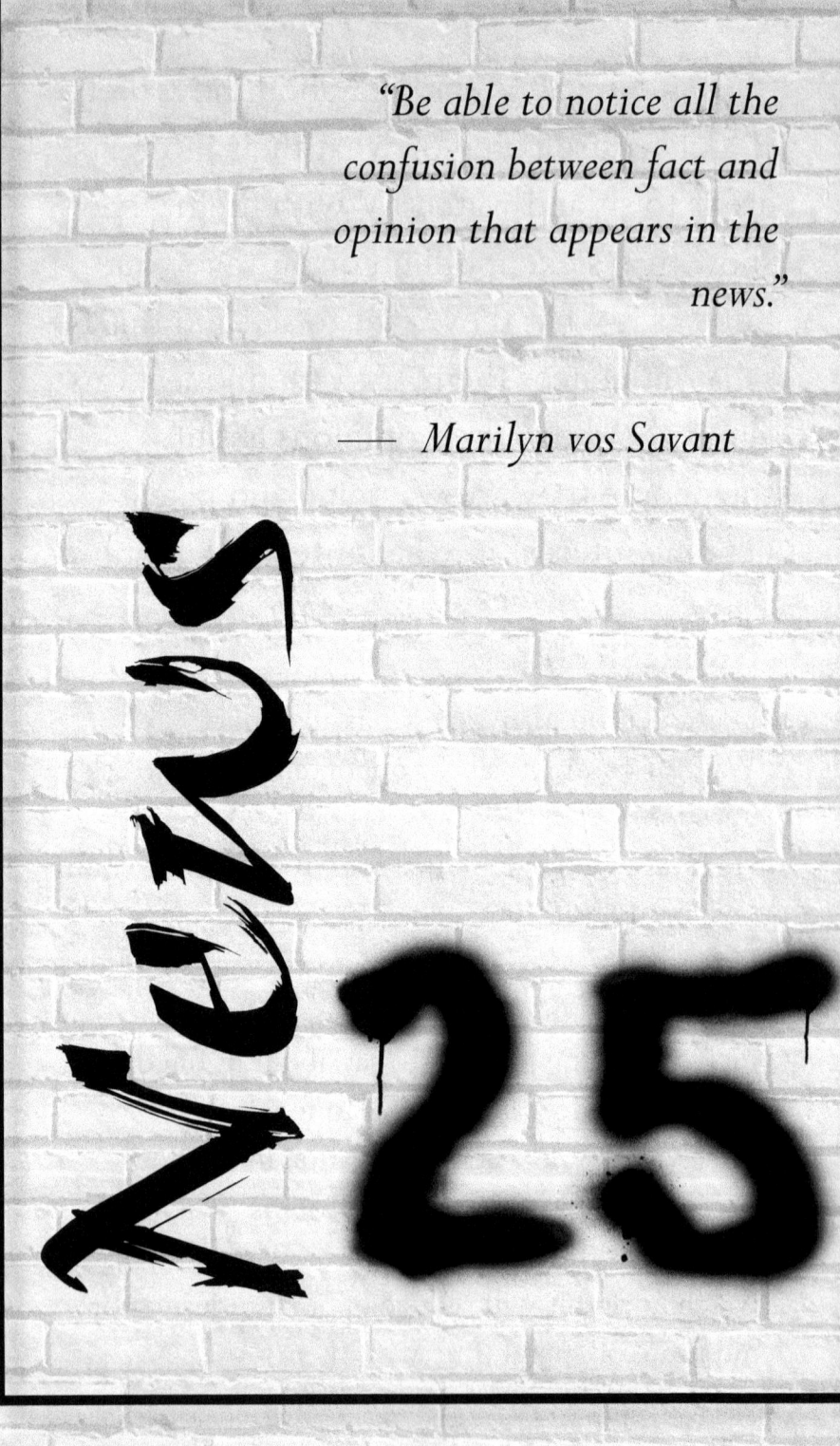

Information and misinformation spreads quickly. Talk to your children about how and where they can get or would hear factual and accurate information. They will hear things and it is more important to teach them where, when and how to access the right information.

Suggestions

- Make sure your children have your contact information and feel comfortable calling you to ask if what they have heard is correct
- Watch the news together and talk openly about the media and how things can be interpreted
- Go over how you would receive information if there was a tragic event that directly impacted your family
- Get a variety of media sources into your home so that your teen can see that these can be opinions as well as information and how stories can be reported very differently.

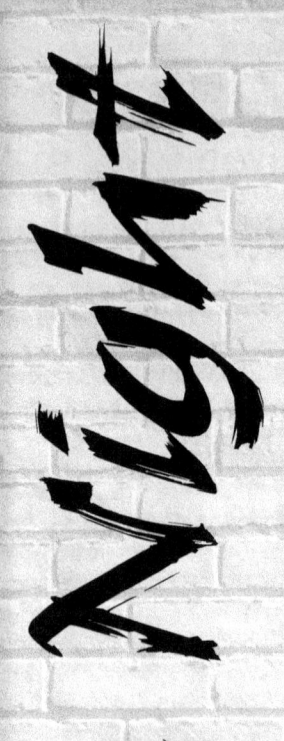

Movie Night

"Movies can and do have tremendous influence in shaping young lives in the realm of entertainment towards the ideals and objectives of normal adulthood."

— Walt Disney

Set aside a night of the week or month when you watch a movie as a family. Watching a movie together is really about spending time together while losing yourselves in something other than your own lives and being entertained while relaxing as a family. It should be an event everyone looks forward to.

Suggestions

- Try to select movies that everyone will enjoy
- Get out blankets, comfy pillows, etc.
- Make sure that everyone has somewhere comfortable to sit
- Turn off cell phones and only answer land line phone if it is urgent and important
- Have a good mix of healthy and loved treats for everyone to enjoy
- Make sure you know what the movie is about and ask the clerk just to confirm it is appropriate for everyone in your family
- Go online and read reviews about movies and get a sense of different movies they would want to rent before leaving the house (it might prevent an argument)

Prioritize

> "The key is not to prioritize what's on your schedule, but to schedule your priorities."
>
> — Stephen Covey

27

Look at what is important to you, and make sure that those are the things you are spending most of your time on. There are plenty of things in our lives that other people think we should consider urgent and important but it is important for you to prioritize and teach your teen how to do the same. Teens need to learn this skill, practice it and have it modeled for them regularly.

Suggestions

- Make a list of the top 10 most important things in your life and then write a list of the top ten things you spend the most time doing. Compare and adjust if necessary
- As a parent, be aware of their priorities so that you can support and remind them when they aren't putting the important things first
- As time passes, priorities will change - make sure to review your lists regularly
- Each Sunday night, review what the week has in store and write as much on a family calendar as possible
- Make sure that the calendar is in a high traffic area or somewhere everyone can see it regularly

Responsibility

"It is easy to dodge our responsibilities, but we cannot dodge the consequences of dodging our responsibilities."

— Josiah Stamp

28

Having responsibilities beyond themselves, and things to get them up in the morning, helps with the sense of being part of something bigger than themselves. It gives their lives more purpose and meaning. Life is filled with responsibility and teaching your teens how to manage them is an essential life skill.

Suggestions

- Find activities that genuinely interest them
- Contact the school to find out if volunteer hours are a mandatory component of their diploma (another motivation)
- Ask them what kind of tasks and responsibilities they want to take on at home, what they would rather not do, and then find a balance
- Try to give everyone an opportunity to discuss any new responsibilities and expectations they will have
- Model being responsible by seeing your commitments through, even when you are tired or unmotivated
- Give them an opportunity to be a leader – contact local community centres and see if they need mentors or homework helpers

Laugh together

"A day without laughter is a day wasted"

— Charlie Chaplin

29

Some days, if you can't laugh, you'll cry. Laughter continues to be considered the best medicine and teens often need an extra dose or two. They can easily get caught up in the stress of life and it is important to show them the lighter side and find things in their day or life that are worthy of some laughter.

Suggestions

- Get a daily calendar that has a joke of the day and tell it to them when you see it
- When they are angry or upset try to point out something humorous that could result from it
- Send them a funny email or picture
- Start meal time with telling them something funny that you heard, saw or did that day
- Go to: www.youtube.com and search for "funny accidents" or "embarrassing moments"
- Buy funny magnets or notepads
- Teach them how to laugh at themselves by making sure you do it once in a while too

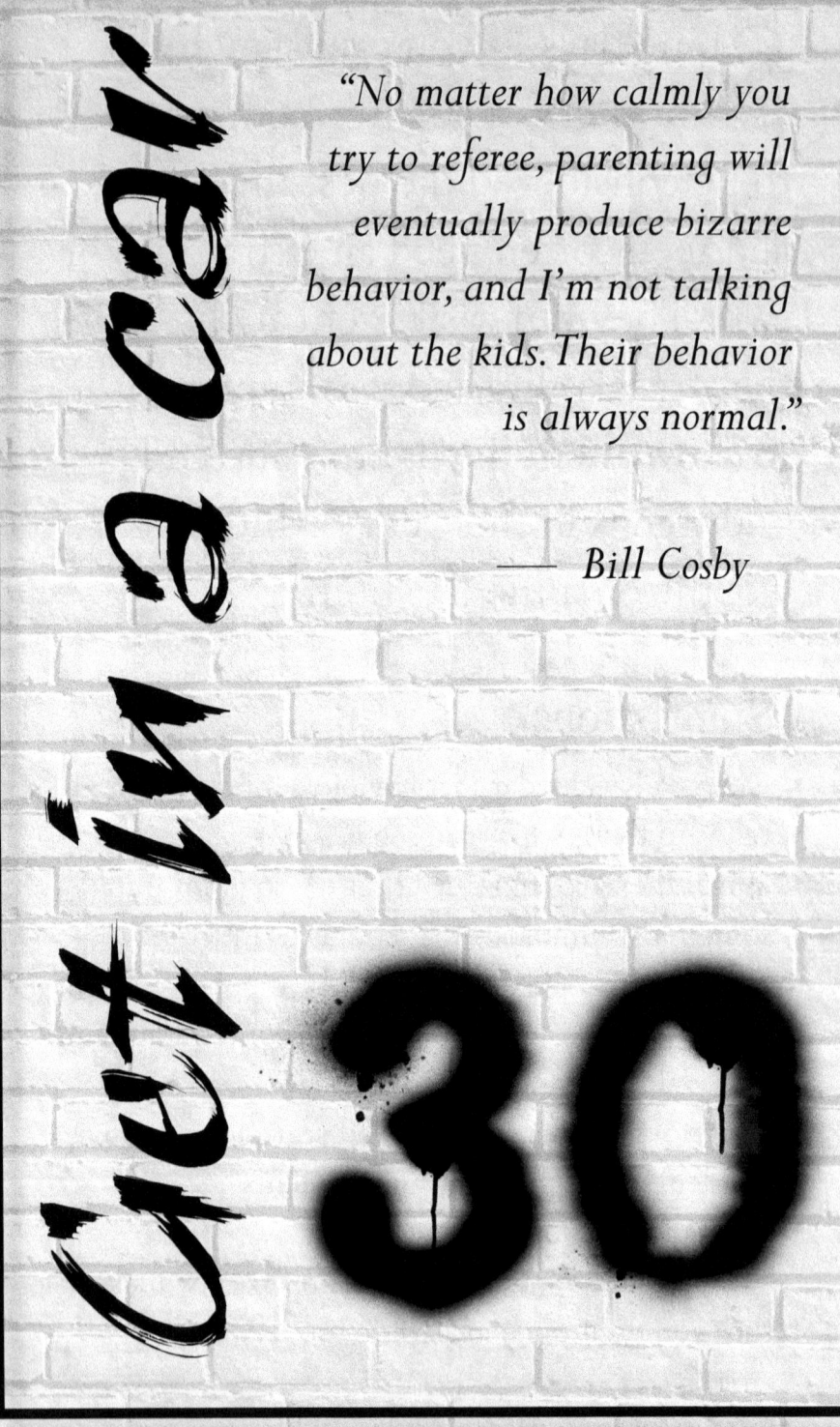

If they won't talk to you, force them. Confine them in the moving car and then take the long route. In a car, it isn't as easy to escape, you don't have to make eye contact (which can make conversation easier for teens), and if you go far enough they don't tend to threaten to get out and walk. The rhythm of the engine or wiper blades can be a relaxant and help to calm even the most hostile of teens.

Suggestions

- Offer to go out for ice cream and take them to a "favourite" spot across town
- Offer to take them to the mall for shoes or a shirt they need and then go to the farthest mall
- Pick them up from an event and run a few errands along the way
- Turn off the radio or ask them to take off any headphones
- Ask questions that need more than a grunt
- Tell them that you need help getting groceries, or some item in and out of the car, or their opinion
- Start with small, 'lighter' topics and listen to their answers to see if you can ask questions that may go deeper

Friends

"Friendships in childhood are usually a matter of chance, whereas in adolescence they are most often a matter of choice."

— *David Elkind*

31

Despite what you may think, you are not completely helpless when it comes to making sure that they choose and keep good friends. Tweens and teens can be good at making and losing friends regularly and their choices can be questionable. There are things you can and should do to encourage and discourage friendships.

Suggestions

- Identify with your children what qualities in a friend you look for and talk about them
- Ask them about their friends (Would you trust them not to do that to you and why?)
- Invite their friends over, be welcoming to all of them (even if it nearly kills you) and make or order meals to keep them there
- Talk about your own bad and good experiences with friends so that they know what your limits were and what theirs should be
- Find an excuse to meet or phone their parents to potentially get another perspective
- Never ban the friend from your house (that alienates) but limit where they go with them
- Avoid getting personal about the person; instead refer to situations that you didn't like

Hobbies

> "A hobby a day keeps the doldrums away."
>
> — Phyllis McGinley

32

Without hobbies, friends can have a bigger influence than you may like. You don't want their only hobbies to be partying, drinking, or playing on a gaming system. Tweens and teens need to be invested in something that keeps them busy and they genuinely like. You don't want to have to force them into something but some gentle encouragement can save you a lot of heartache.

Suggestions

- Think about all of the things they are good at or interested in, the classes at school they 'like' more than others, etc.
- Find out about local groups, get information about clubs or courses BEFORE asking them about it so that you can see if it fits in your schedule and budget
- Suggest the hobby with another friend who also might be interested in taking part or encourage them to get involved
- Find out what age group and gender also participate (this can really influence their decision making)
- Try out as many things as you need to and ask only that they make some type of commitment (try it for 3 sessions, 2 weeks, 1 month, etc.)

keep them busy

"I am always busy, which is perhaps the chief reason why I am always well."

— Elizabeth Cady Stanton

33

Most tweens and teens get into trouble when they have time on their hands or are bored. Don't fill their schedules so full that they barely have time to eat or watch the occasional movie or TV show but enough so that they don't have hours on end of unsupervised, unstructured, boredom time.

Suggestions
- Help them to find a healthy balance between school, friends, activities and responsibilities
- If they spend over 3 hours a night on the phone, watching TV, playing or chatting on the computer or using a gaming system then they have too much time on their hands
- Look into sports and recreational activities to get them off the couch and meeting new people
- Do something as a family together (bike rides, horseback riding, yard work, renovating, board games, tennis, skating, going to the library, etc.)
- Sign them up for lessons or courses that will get them additional qualifications and begin developing skills that will look good on a resume (swim qualifications, babysitting course, first aid course, etc.)

Feelings

> "Do not think that love, in order to be genuine, has to be extraordinary. What we need is to love without getting tired."
>
> — *Mother Teresa*

34

Find a balance between being honest and open but not treating them like a friend instead of your child. If sharing your feelings will add to their stress levels, ask yourself if you need to share this with them for their own good, or just yours. It is important to teach your teens about sharing feelings but also doing it for the right reasons, at the appropriate times and in appropriate ways.

Suggestions

- Think before you speak to them — unless it is urgent and important take some time to think about what, where, when and how you are going to share your feelings
- Use other people as a sounding board - ask a trusted friend or family member first
- Tweens and teens can cycle through a lot of emotions and feelings in one day - try to have them work on identifying facts vs. feelings
- Don't be secretive or hide your feelings. It is healthy to express your feelings and when you express emotions and responses to events, you are teaching your children how to express themselves
- Don't talk about deep feelings every day — it can be overwhelming and will appear less genuine

Be Consistent

"Our children are counting on us to provide two things: consistency and structure. Children need parents who say what they mean, mean what they say, and do what they say they are going to do."

— *Barbara Coloroso*

35

Your children should know your answer before they have asked the question. It won't stop them from asking the question, but be predictable and make sure you give the consistent answer. Teens thrive on consistency and sometimes rely on it. Ever had your teen ask you a question in front of their friends that you just can't believe they would even bother asking? They are often looking to you to tell their friends where you stand, and give them an excuse not to have to do it.

Suggestions

- Be consistent and fair – when you say no, mean it and make sure you are saying no because it is in their best interests
- Try to avoid answering difficult questions 'on the spot'
- Answer some question with, "What do you think I am going to say?" - it can be interesting to hear their thinking
- When you make your decision, make sure you are heard clearly, don't repeat it over and over again, and offer further consequences if they continue to harass you
- Physically move out of their sight, go for a drive, or get on the phone with someone who will support and strengthen you

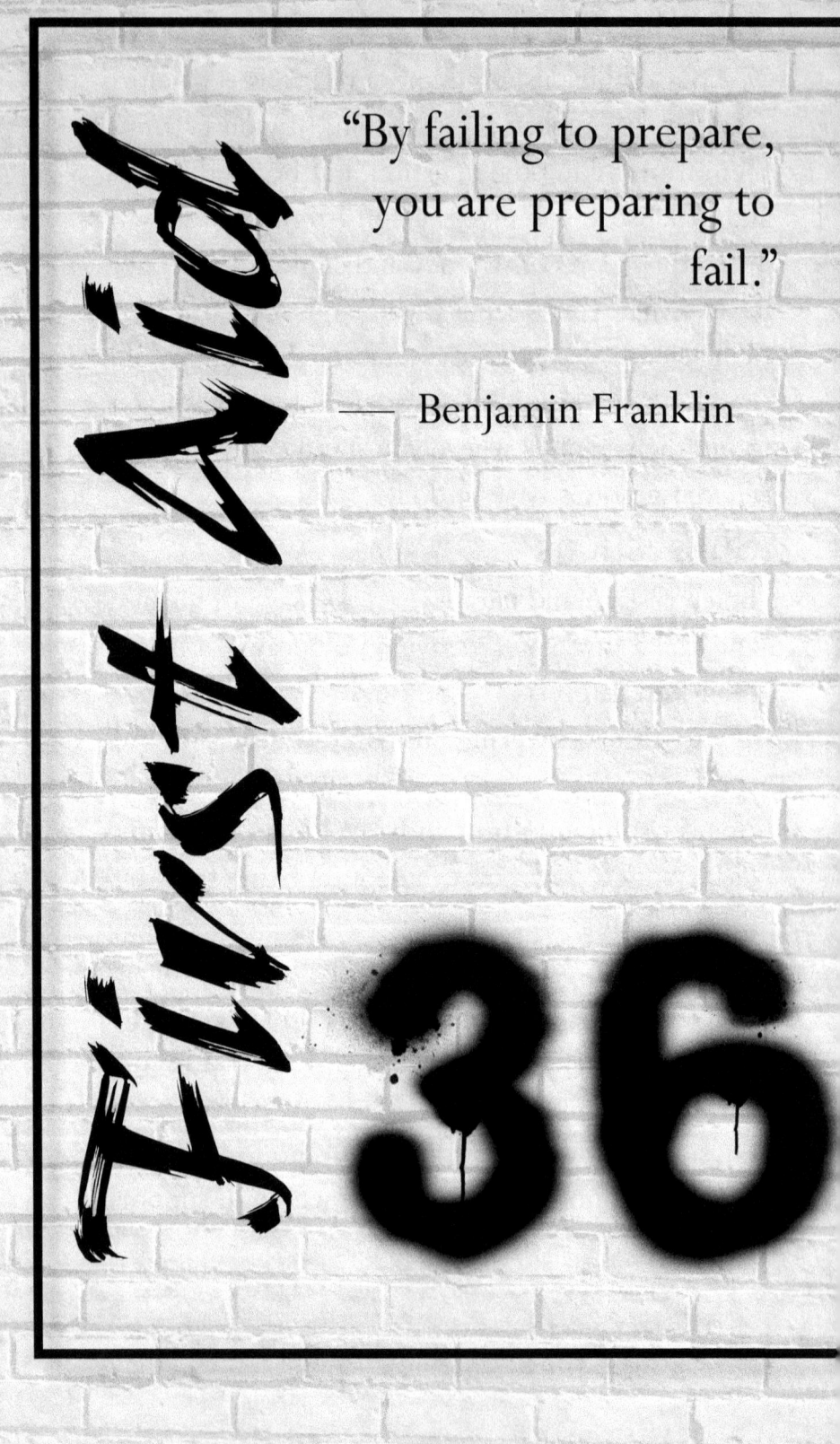

Having a first aid kit in your home and car is a good way to provide a little extra peace of mind and ensures you have some basics should the need ever arrive for either yourself or your teens. Most stores sell pre-packaged kits, or you can make your own.

Suggestions
- Check it regularly to ensure things have not been "borrowed" and need replacing
- Go through it with your family so they know what it does and doesn't have
- Go to the Canadian or American Red Cross website for a list of things to have in a first aid kit
- Keep it in an easy to access area and where everyone can find it
- Check items for expiry dates
- Ensure you are storing the kit where it will stay at a consistent temperature and dry
- Include a list of contact information in a ziplock bag with the kit

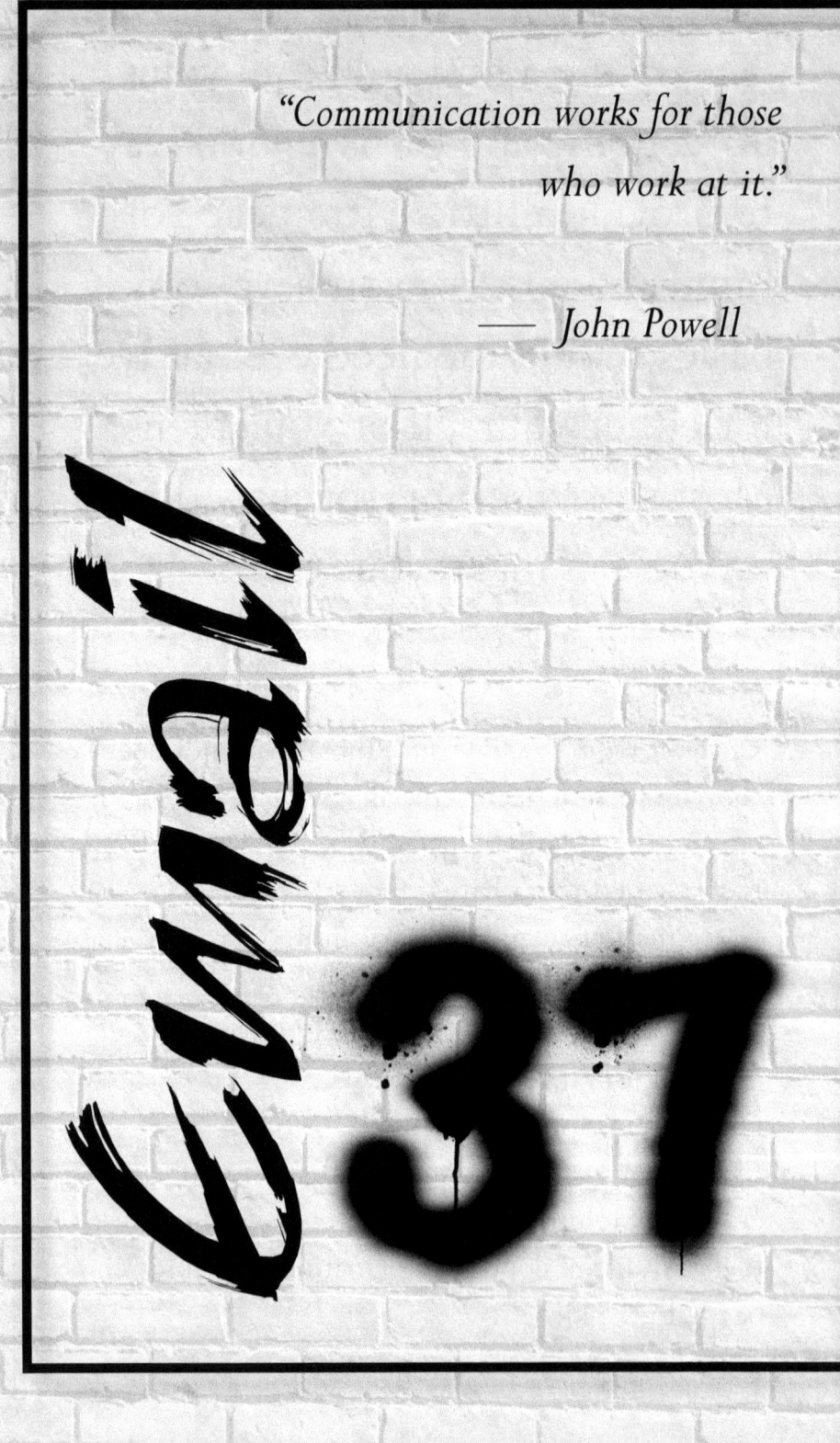

If communication is difficult, email or text them! Send them a daily note, joke or picture to let them know that you are thinking of them and want to keep the lines of communication open. Use any method possible to get into their daily lives and tell them that you love them; they may never say they appreciate it but they will and do.

Suggestions
- Be careful when writing as your words can often be misinterpreted when they don't have your facial expressions, gestures and tone to also help interpret your message
- Encourage face to face communication in your email (ex: Would you like to go for ice cream tonight?)
- Attach a funny picutre of yourself or the family
- Don't react to emails by writing back immediately – if you are upset or uncertain about an email, call or speak face to face whenever possible
- Have the computer in a central location so you can glance regularly at what is going on

"*We are made kind by being kind*"

— Eric Hoffer

cards 38

Sometimes Hallmark really does say it best! While I am sure your tween or teen gets cards for birthdays or other special occassions, it is also a nice way of connecting with them to say that you love them, are proud of who they are or think they are terrific at random times throughout the year.

Suggestions
- Buy a box of cards for all occasions – this would be a time saver
- Make checking the cards a monthly routine so they are not forgotten
- Get extra cards for silly, special or significant times
- Leave a card under a pillow or in the bathroom in the morning to start and/or finish a day
- Give your teen a few blank cards that are already addressed for them to write and give to others when they feel like it

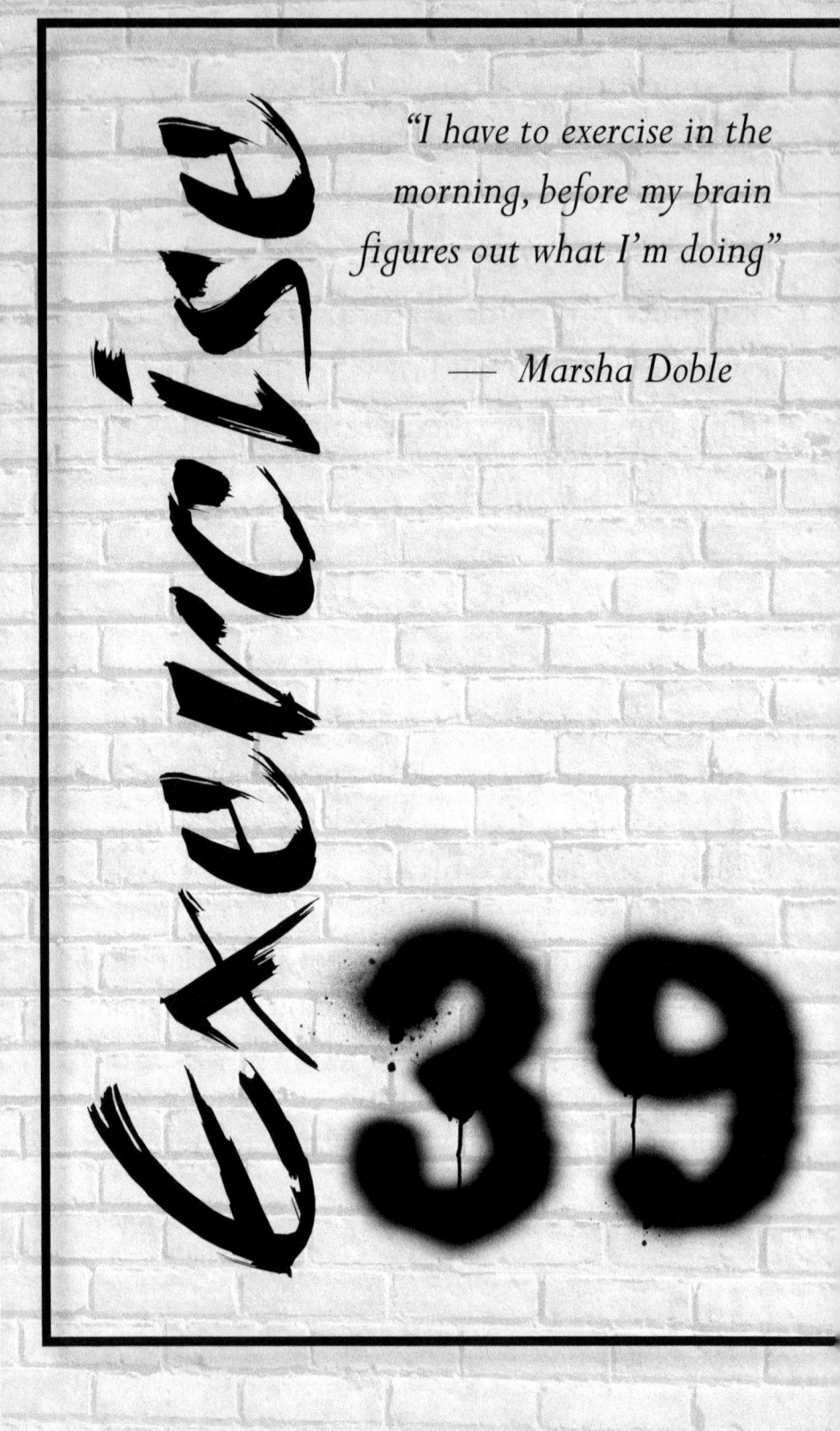

In order to feel good both mentally and physically your children need exercise. You cannot rely on their school to give it to them. Your teen should be getting a minimum of 45 minutes of exercise 5 days a week. Exercise has been known to not only to help combat moodiness, anxiety and depression but also gives them more energy and an increased level of confidence and a better self image.

Suggestions

- Find something you can do as a family at least once a week
- If they don't enjoy the exercise they are doing, find something else they will enjoy
- Look into the extracurricular school programs that are offered and contact the teacher in charge to see if they could approach or encourage your child to participate
- Buy equipment to have at your house so there are no excuses
- If they are on a team or participate in activities be sure to attend regularly to show your support
- Model the behaviour, it is hard for your children to be inspired if you are saying it from the couch
- Find out what sports teams their friends are on and get your tweens/teens involved too

Family meetings

> *"If you can keep your head when all about you are losing theirs, it's just possible you haven't grasped the situation."*
>
> — Jean Kerr

40

You don't need to label what they are, but you should be meeting with everyone in your family at least once a week. You can do it over dinner or whenever you have them all gathered together. Touching base about what is working, what isn't, what is happening both in and out of the house is a great way to prevent confusion, chaos and freak outs.

Suggestions

- Have a calendar out so that you can talk about the week ahead and mark any significant commitments or dates onto it
- Allow each person a chance to speak, without being interrupted
- Take notes about issues so that you can follow up with them, if necessary
- Don't make them long meetings that go on forever about issues and annoyances – the idea is to organize your family and prevent issues or problems from occurring throughout the week
- Meetings should be between 10 – 20 minutes
- Prioritize what you want to talk about by having a list of points you want to cover
- If bigger issues come up, plan a specific time to address them and then get back on track

Music and Movies

> "When you see a rattlesnake poised to strike, you do not wait until he has struck before you crush him."
>
> — Franklin D. Roosevelt

Watch what they are watching and listen to their IPODs. Not only is it important to take an interest in their taste of music, favourite internet sites and movies but these are the things that influence their thinking and you need to have an opportunity to challenge these views and ideologies and offer other perspectives and ideas (you can't do this if you don't know what is influencing them) and how).

Suggestions

- "Borrow" their MP3 player, CDs, listen to the music on their computer
- Don't forget your sense of humour, if you are going to challenge someone else's views try to do it with humour
- Avoid making judgements and getting personal, stick to using phrases like; "In my opinion…", "I think that their lyrics are…", "Did you hear what they said in that song about…" etc.
- Look up the movies that they want to go and see or rent and see what other people said about them
- Choose your battles for the big things and avoid getting caught up on little issues that keep you from discussing bigger ones

information sessions

"Start by doing the necessary, then the possible, and suddenly you are doing the impossible"

— Francis of Assisi

42

If your school or community centre is offering information sessions go to them - information is power. Drag your tweens and teens with you; hearing information from another source, sadly, gives it more credibility than if you just said it. They may pretend to be annoyed, disinterested or bored but they are listening and may get answers to questions they didn't even know they had, ideas of how to be more involved with the community or at school.

Suggestions

- Make it a required family event
- Call ahead to make sure it is age appropriate for them
- Ask to be included on any emailing lists or contact information so that you can get regular updates or information about things being offered
- Use their websites and check them regularly to see what sessions are offered and when, or any changes that may have occurred
- Get names of people you could contact to get more information if it was ever needed
- Take their leaflets, information sheets, handouts, etc. and make a file at home for them, so you know where they are should you need them

You will never regret having an emergency car kit in each of your cars, particularly if your child is driving. It puts your mind at ease and can help prevent more serious incidences from occurring. 'Be prepared' should be your family motto for all car journeys as you never know what can happen.

Suggestions
- AAA or CAA is useful to have especially when one of your family members is absent. It will give you piece of mind.
- Buy a pre-made emergency kit for your car
- If making your own kit it should include: candles, matches, empty gas can, shovel, emergency blankets, battery or windup radio, jumper cables, first aid kit, energy bars, water, etc.
- Google emergency car kits for more information
- Make a rule that having the car always means you get to know their destination and approximate timings
- Make the "call me" rule - no matter what time, where you are or if you think I'll be angry.

Natural Consequences

> *"A problem is a chance for you to do your best"*
>
> — Duke Ellington

Make the punishment fit the crime. If you go overboard and strip everything away you'll only end up punishing yourself and making your relationship even more stressful. Find out what they value and hold them accountable for their actions, but don't take everything, or you'll have nothing to bargain with when the next incident occurs (and there will definitely be a next incident).

Suggestions

- If it is the car they took without permission then keep it to a punishment involving the car
- If it is using the internet inappropriately then put a lock on it for a few weeks and look into safety settings; if it is done again – take away all directly unsupervised internet access for a month and warn that the third strike will be a complete ban for several months
- If there is a respect issue in how they are speaking to you then stop doing things for them
- Issues at school should also have a consequence at home, regardless of whether or not the school has already given a consequence (ex: cheating on a test – ask school to send home project or additional assignment that will be done in their "free" time)

Realistic Expectations

"Often the difference between a successful person and a failure is not one's better abilities or ideas, but the courage that one has to bet on one's ideas, to take a calculated risk – and to act"

— Andre Malraux

Keep your expectations clear, realistic and attainable. Your child is constantly dealing with the changes and curve balls that tween and teen life throws at them. It is important that you have high expectations for your teens but not so high that they are unattainable or unrealistic. This will drive a bigger wedge between you and your child and cause hurt feelings, frustration and anger. Set the bar just high enough that they can touch it with their finger tips.

Suggestions
- Keep your expectations realistic by talking regularly with your teen about what they fear, love, want, need, etc.
- Talk to teachers and others about your teens, your expectations and get their opinions
- Listen when they tell you your expectations are too high and then you will need to decide whether they are frightened, unmotivated, discouraged, unwilling or just need someone to believe in them
- Make sure that they are challenged but not overwhelmed – you want your teen to feel as though you believe in them, not that they are a disappointment to you

Cell Phone & Features

> "Be aware of the ways in which they see and experience the world or they'll run circles around you."
> — *Megan Egerton*

Know what is on their cell phone, contacts, features and passwords. They live under your roof, eat your food and they want the PRIVILEGE of a cell phone then they abide by your rules. Privacy happens when they move out!

Suggestions

- No text messaging or phone calls during meals or other specified family times
- Cell phones are charged in the living room or kitchen at night
- There should be no expectation of privacy – if you are going to read it, go through it, etc. tell them (not when, but that you will)
- Invest in call display as it makes screening calls much easier, and the reverse – when it is you calling, they pick up or they lose the phone
- Find out what school policies around the phone are, and make sure they adhere to them
- Get regular updates of their contacts – their friends are your business
- Remind your teen that a cell phone is a privilege – misuse it and you lose it, even if they are paying the bill (your house, your rules)

Hours of Operation

> "Forget past mistakes. Forget failures. Forget everything except what you're going to do now and do it"
>
> — Will Durant

47

Don't only find out where they are going but take the time to research the place's hours of operation. This not only ensures you will see through any possible 'alternate plan' but also that your child doesn't wind up outside of somewhere, late at night, in an unsafe situation.

Suggestions

- Ask where they are going and when they are going to be there
- Find out how they are getting from A to B and back again
- Remind them that they can call you and if you aren't available give them another person to call
- Call the places they are going to and ask their hours of operation before they leave
- Ensure they have a way of contacting you if plans change
- Find out the location of where they are going and what approximate travel times will be

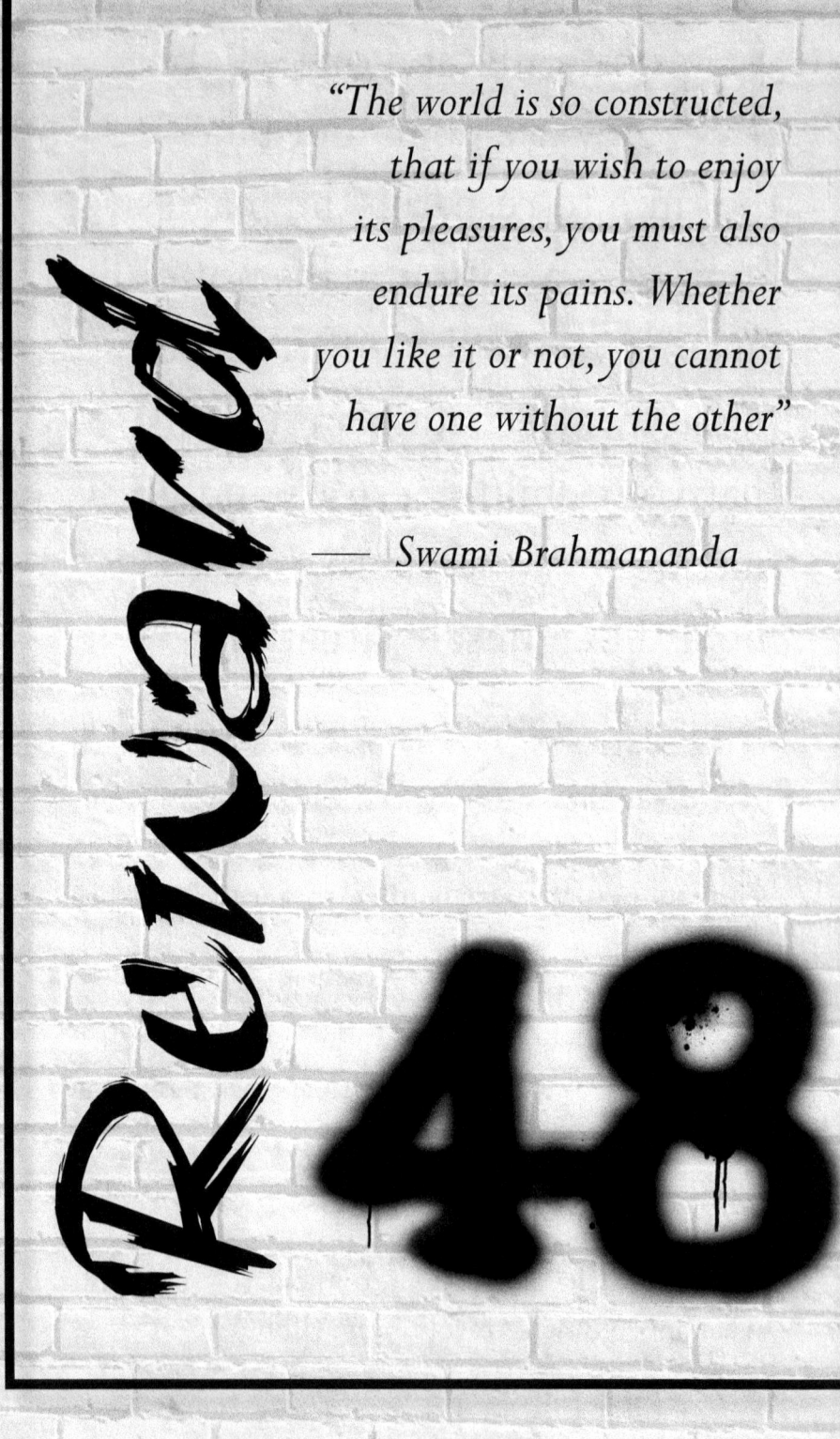

Life is full of rewards – rewards for finding something, winning something, learning something, etc. Everyone gets rewarded, in some way, for doing things well or surviving difficult situations or circumstances. Don't forget to reward your teens for enduring, thriving or just surviving teen life.

Suggestions

- Reward them with your time
- You don't have to spend a ton of money on a teen – it can be their favourite dessert, ordering a pizza, renting a movie, taking them to a movie and watching it with them
- Make a big deal out of choices that they make – not to drink and drive, coming home early to study, helping out around the house
- Ask your family to make a list of things that they would consider rewards, then you can be certain you are really rewarding them

Take as many pictures as you can get away with, as often as you can. Having photos around the house and in their "spaces" is a constant reminder of happy times, the people that they love and love them.

Suggestions

- Have different people take photos so you will be sure to get different perspectives, people, etc.
- Get photos printed regularly and then put them up on the fridge, cork board, bathroom door, bedrooms, etc.
- Have a photo of the week and send it to family and friends living futher away
- Take regular photos so they can see their changes and a realistic picture of what they look like – take ones of them in different settings, moods or clothes
- Remember that if you are posting pictures on the web be prepared for anyone to see them

"Of all the roles I've played, none has been as fulfilling as being a mother."

— *Annette Funicello*

If you are on a tight budget or just feel like being creative this is a great way to show your tween or teen that you appreciate the things you do and are going to give them an opportunity to "cash in". Making an IOU booklet also gives you a chance to reflect on all of the responsibilities different family members have and don't always get recognized for doing.

Suggestions

- Make a booklet for each family member
- Don't forget to make rules like only one can be cashed a week or only one family member a day – otherwise you may end up being worn out and run off your feet
- Make a list of all the things they do to get an idea of what things you want to help out with and include things that would be easy for you to accomplish or have happen
- IOU – breakfast in bed, nag free night, morning off school, dishes free pass, laundry fluffed and folded, walk the dog, ride to school, etc.

Screen Savers 51

> *"If you haven't found something strange during the day, it hasn't been much of a day."*
>
> — J.A. Wheeler

Since tweens and teens spend a good portion of their time, whether it is for their school work or social lives, on the computer, it can be a good place to put notes, pictures, reminders, suggestions and not so subtle hints on any computers in the house. Use your computers to your advantage and quickly learn how to make a new screen saver.

Suggestions
- Insert funny pictures every now and again
- Make reminder notes about commitments or events coming up
- Use family photos to create a slideshow screen saver
- Go to Google and search for instructions on how to make a screen saver
- Spend time with your teen by getting them to show you how to do it
- Keep your notes brief, light and easy to read and interpret
- Use Google Images to find funny or silly pictures

Make videos

> "What do we live for if not to make life less difficult for each other?"
>
> — George Eliot

52

Make some videos as a personal and special way to say congratulations, or I am so proud of you. They will then be around for years to watch and remind your teens of the family they are a part of, their achievements, talents, abilities, etc.

Suggestions

- Make sure you watch them through first before sharing them with other friends and family
- Make sure family members take turns taking the video so that the same person isn't always absent from the screen
- Have the camera out so that you remember to bring it to events or special occassions
- Make rules around your teens using the video camera and make sure your expectations are clear

Say "I love you"

53

> "We can do no great things — only small things with great love"
>
> — Mother Teresa

Saying you love your teen, even when you don't like them very much, is important and needs to be done daily. With tweens and teens it isn't enough to show you love them, you have to say it too. They need to hear it even when you are disappointed in them or frustrated with their decisions. They may look at you like you are crazy but they need this affirmation. Make sure you say it often and genuinely (they can sniff out when you aren't being genuine).

Suggestions

- Never say "I love you" in anger – people can interpret this as just something you say without thought, and when you say it later, in different circumstances, they won't believe it
- Say it daily and make eye contact with the person when you say it and say the actual words
- Don't embarrass them by saying it over and over again in front of others
- Don't say it expecting or waiting to hear it back
- Say it at different moments and times in the day so it won't feel it is a scheduled thing that is just another part of your routine or day
- When you say it, offer reasons why you feel the way you do
- If this is hard for you try using it as a conversation closer – when they are about to hang up, leave for school, get out of the car, etc.

Surprise your family, tween or teen when you can see they just needs a boost. Often teens can get caught up in the day to day routine or drama that is their lives and they need a surprise every now and again to remind them that they won't always see the good things coming their way.

Suggestions

- Put $5 with a post it note in their wallet or purse that says treat yourself
- Get their favourite junk food, rent a movie and have a night off from life
- Put their favourite type of magazine on their pillow for when they go to bed
- Fill up the car with gas and leave a post-it saying something like, 'because I love you'
- Give them the night off of dishes for no reason
- Put a gift certificate or IOU coupon under their plate at dinner
- Drive them to school one day and stop for their favourite treat along the way
- Leave candies in funny places all over the house
- Make a series of clues that will eventually lead to something that they weren't expecting

Unbirthdays

> "The way I see it, you should live everyday like it's your birthday."
>
> — Paris Hilton

55

Everyone needs an excuse to have a party or celebrate. Have an "unbirthday" party with cake, a gift, favourite restaurant, a card, etc. Making life a little lighter and less predictable keeps your teens on their toes and reminds them about all the things there are to celebrate or be grateful for (at the least they can be grateful you are so thoughtful!).

Suggestions

- Make it on a night of the week that doesn't have other things scheduled so that you are not rushed
- Take pictures and if family members are deployed or away – email them photos of you having fun so they worry less
- If the thought of organizing something like this overwhelms you, ask a friend, relative or neighbour to help out, or have it at their place
- Write them a "just because" card and tell them all the things you admire about them
- If you are on a tight budget don't go overboard – spending time together and the card are the most important things

"Change will not come if we wait for some other person or some other time. We are the ones we've been waiting for. We are the change that we seek."

— *Barack Obama*

Teach them how to adapt to and make the most of change. Change happens everyday whether or not we want it to. They need to learn about how changes can become opportunities. The better your teen is at adapting to change, the better equipped they will be overall to handle anything life throws their way.

Suggestions
- Help your children to see that change is constant, everywhere and unavoidable
- Model accepting changes – new schools, new teachers, new friends
- Talk about changes that have already happened and the good things that have come because of it
- Discuss physical vs. emotional changes, changes you can see and some you don't
- Keep growth charts and take photos regularly so that you will be able to see the physical changes over the months that you don't always see when you are living with someone

Learn Something New

"All life is an experiment. The more experiments you make the better."

— Ralph Waldo Emerson

Join a club, take a course together, have them teach you something; just spend time together learning something new. When you agree to take on a course or learn something, you are teaching them that you are never too old to learn. It also helps if you are in the same boat and learning something together – it may even be the source of a lot of laughter!

Suggestions
- Get a variety of options to choose from
- Choose something that is close and convenient and won't be another chore or obligation you don't need
- Choose a night that both of you have relatively nothing that's time consuming or urgently needs doing on the following day – you want to be 100% in the moment not worrying about the next day's commitments
- Let your teen have input about the day of the week and the timings
- When choosing an activity, think about what you want to get out of it, how many weeks it goes for. Have realistic expectations and make sure it is something that isn't going to add stress

Give Praise

"If you want your children to improve, let them overhear the nice things you say about them to others"

— *Haim Ginott*

58

Acknowledge the milestones and accomplishments to ensure they know you are proud of them, you recognize their hard work and efforts and that you value their achievements. Teens may need to hear the same praise at least two or three times before they even consider believing it.

Suggestions

- Give praise regularly
- Make sure you explain why you feel the way you do
- Don't let them shrug it off easily, ask them if they are proud of themselves and then why or why not
- Show them you are proud by displaying any certificates, projects, awards prominently in your home
- Take a picture of the moment telling them you want to remember it forever and they should too
- If they truly don't like big productions made about their achievements, get them a card, that tells them how impressed or proud you are, and leave it on their pillow

59

Eat together

> "You create opportunities by asking for them."
>
> —— *Patty Hansen*

Make eating one meal a day together a family requirement. Eating together, even just once a day, is important as it is a time you can touch base, and share thoughts, ideas, tears and laughter as a family. Making the commitment to eat together is easy; not letting life getting in the way of that commitment is the challenge.

Suggestions

- Do not answer the phone during meals or explain you're eating dinner and will call back
- All cell phones are turned off or unanswered
- Meals should be at roughly the same time every night so there can be no excuse about not knowing what time dinner is
- Try and get everyone in the family involved in meal planning so you don't have to hear; 'We never eat things I like'
- Use this opportunity to ask questions about their day and don't accept a grunt or yes/no answer
- Use 'conversation starters' and place the cards under their plates to help generate important discussions (got to: www.wywa.org for printable conversation cards)

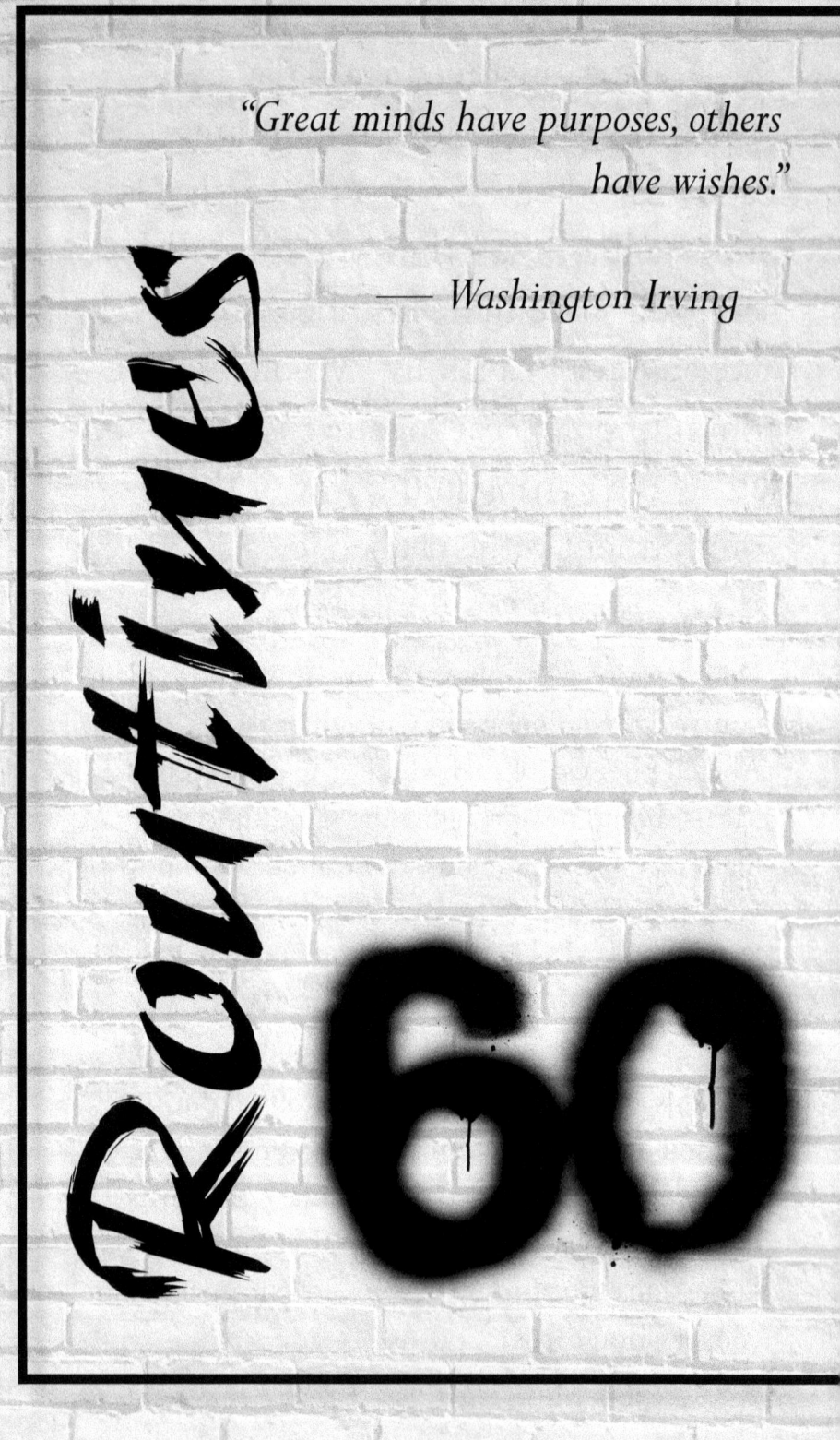

"Great minds have purposes, others have wishes."

— Washington Irving

Routines

60

Teens can really thrive on a certain amount of routine and predictability. During times of significant changes or stress make sure you maintain as many of your routines and family rituals that you can. Teens will look to you to provide them with some sameness, sanity and predictability. Create a life for them that is routine based with surprises thrown in.

Suggestions
- Keep meal times at a consistent time
- If you have family rituals or special events that are always done at certain times of the day, week, month or year, try to maintain the important ones
- Have set times to complete chores, homework, tasks, etc., this way the expectations and time limits are clear and set
- Don't get so caught up in creating routine that you forget to have some fun, but create enough so that your teens feel like they are coming home to a house where they have a good sense of what is happening throughout the week
- Ask each family member to talk about the routines they think are working and ones they would love to change or get rid of

Network of support

> "Service to others is the rent you pay for living on this planet"
>
> —Marian Wright Edelman

Just as you need people around you or available to you when times are stressful, fun, tiring, or awful, so do your teens. Talk to them about the people they would go to or talk to in certain situations and make sure they know how and when to contact them and listen to the reasons why they chose them.

Suggestions

- Don't be offended if you aren't named as part of their support system – it is assumed, if not stated
- Make sure everyone can access the contact information for everyone they consider support
- Your children should know all of your contact information and how to reach you at any time
- Give your children information about who to contact in an emergency and leave that information on the fridge or other central and easy to access area of your home
- Send out an email to everyone on your list so that they have each other's information
- If you are someone else's support – let your teen know this so that if an important call comes through they know to give you the message

Make lists

> "Each day comes bearing its own gifts, untie the ribbons."
> — Ruth Ann Schabacker

62

Create lists of things that your family is interested in, currently doing, wishes for, wants, needs, etc. This keeps your family dreaming, goal setting, talking and exchanging thoughts and ideas in a light way. The lists can help to start conversations and debates, prioritizing needs, sharing in a fun way. You can learn a lot about your teen based on their lists.

Suggestions
1. 10 things you want to do before your 18 years old
2. Top 5 jobs you would never want to do
3. Top 20 songs you think should never be sung by _____
4. 10 Ten things you would say to _____
5. Top 5 favourite foods
6. The worst things about life right now
7. 10 best movies ever made
8. Best things to do on a Saturday
9. 5 best things about school
10. 10 things that annoy me the most

"I do not want the peace which passeth understanding, I want the understanding which bringeth peace."

— Helen Keller

Respect

63

Demand respect and model it. If you don't want them to yell, freak out, scream or otherwise disrespect you, then you shouldn't do it either. They are looking for signs of hypocrisy and this is an area you should never give it to them. Your tweens and teens need to know that you respect them as people. They are looking to you as a gauge in how they should treat others and let others treat them. Do not tolerate their disrespect. One of your many jobs is to teach your teens how you want to be treated and how you want them to be treated.

Suggestions

- End all conversations that begin with raised voices, tone and/or attitude but state the specific time when you will come back to it
- Never have a conversation in anger
- Identify what you find disrespectful and why
- Do not ignore disrespect, it doesn't go away – if you don't like the way they are talking to you or treating you, calmly and clearly tell them
- Watch how you talk about, and to, other people – they are watching you for direction
- If their friends are disrespectful, address it directly with their friends – you must set and adhere to standards in your home
- Model respect by actively listening to their opinions, perceptions and ideas

Volunteer

"Be of service. Whether you make yourself available to a friend or co-worker, or you make time every month to do volunteer work, there is nothing that harvests more of a feeling of empowerment than being of service to someone in need."

— *Gillian Anderson*

64

Teens are quite self-centred by nature and volunteering is a great way to get them to step out of their worlds and experience other realities. Volunteering for people less fortunate than themselves can help them to appreciate what they have. Volunteering for something can also provide them with a sense of purpose, and being needed and wanted can be intoxicating. At the least, it is a great way to build an impressive resume, and keeps them from being bored.

Suggestions

- Match your teen's skills and interests with a volunteer position
- Get a list of volunteer possibilities in your community to help them find something that will be of interest to them
- Have your child make a commitment for a certain period of time
- Talk about the experience with them and support this endeavour whenever possible (with rides to and from, new outfit to work in, etc.)
- Ask at your local community centre on the base if there are things that your teen could help with or get involved with

Ask for help

> "Some days you're the bug. Some days you're a windshield"
>
> — Price Cobb

65

Teens are not psychic and often are so self-absorbed that they wouldn't notice the roof caving in so… if you want help, you have to ask. You should not have to ask over and over again but you definitely need to say it directly and out loud if you want something done. Hints are too subtle and asking over and over again gets them irritated – find the medium.

Suggestions

- Don't ask for too much at once
- Be specific
- Talk when there is no distraction and you are certain they heard you
- Look at what is most important to you and prioritize for demands
- Make sure you are not always asking the same people in your family
- Give them a time frame for when you would like something done and the consequences if it isn't completed within that time frame (i.e. if you don't dust the house by Friday then I will have to do it, and if I am busy doing that then I won't be able to take you and your friends to baseball)
- Ask them to go over, in their own words, what they think you are asking them to do

Hire someone

"Now is no time to think of what you do not have. Think of what you can do with what there is"

— Ernest Hemingway

66

Life can be busy at certain times in the year for your tween or teen. If you can afford to hire someone to cut the lawn, shovel the driveway or walk the dog once a month, give your teen that break. Being a teen is a lot of work and they will appreciate the occasional break from the responsibility and you'll enjoy the nagging break too.

Suggestions

- Offer one of their friends the job – that way the friend is over and you are giving your child a break
- Find a neighbourhood child who is willing to do it every now and again
- Take a flyer or advertise at the local high school
- Hire someone to clean the house, rake the lawn, paint the fence and treat yourself to a nag free experience, and enjoy actually getting it done the way you like or want
- If they have younger siblings that they babysit, hire a sitter and take them out to a movie or dinner
- See if there is something you can trade for (i.e. If I hire you to cut my grass you can hire me to repair your lawnmower)

Use Paper Plates

> "Housework can't kill you, but why take a chance?"
>
> —— *Phyllis Diller*

67

Make a few meals easier. Life is busy and demands on your family's time is always changing. Teens will definitely appreciate it when they have fewer chores and responsibilities. One meal a week, use paper plates and avoid having dishes. Making meals easier for your teens also translates into less work for parents, too, and fewer arguments about who is doing the dishes.

Suggestions
- Assign a particular night a week when meals will be simple and 'dishless'
- Have a competition to see who can make the tastiest meal with the least amount of dishes
- Be environmentally friendly and only use biodegradable paper plates and cups
- Take your disposable dinner to the park or outside to make even less mess in your house and you'll have more interesting surroundings
- If you know of another family struggling at meal time, take your mess-free meal to their house – misery loves company and you'll feel good helping someone else out with their meals

Send Flowers

"Flowers always make people better, happier, and more helpful; they are sunshine, food and medicine for the soul."

— Luther Burbank

Flowers some times can say it better than you can. Sending flowers can tell your teen that they arevalued and cherished. These surprises keep teens on their toes and since it is usually always the other way around, this is a good thing.

Suggestions

- Don't wait for a special occasion, make one up or just include a card that says something along the lines of; 'Because you are you'
- Make sure they are being sent to somewhere that won't overly embarrass them – if you are having them delivered at their school or place of work make sure this isn't going to upset them
- Always sign the card, even if you use a secret code – this way your teen isn't thinking they were from someone else and misunderstandings don't occur

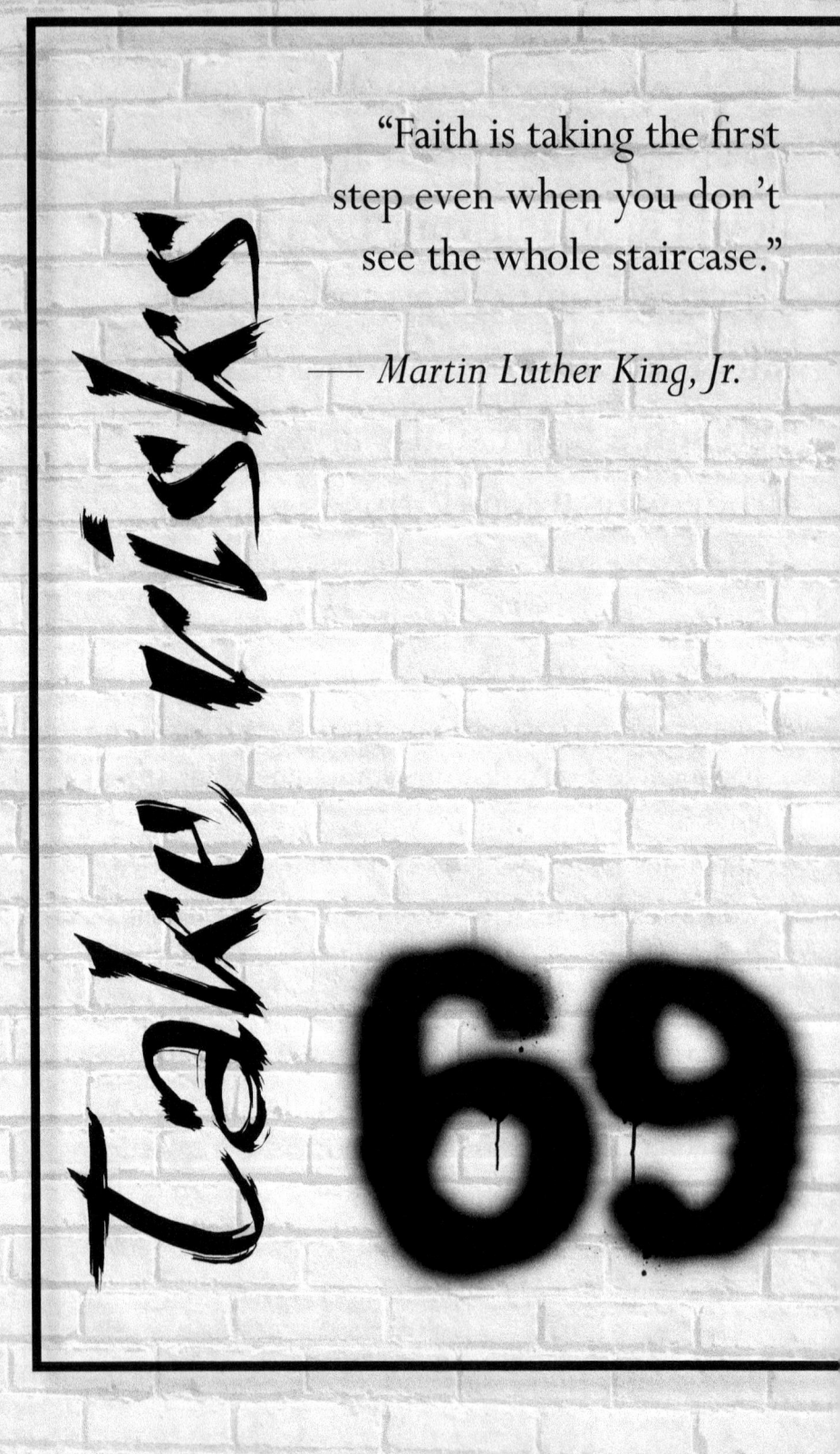

Life is full of opportunities that can be risky. Some of the best opportunities for teens can occur when they step out of their 'comfort zone' and take a risk. It is essential for you to encourage this and model it. Risk taking means that there will be failures and successes, but they will experience neither if they don't try. Often teens are worried about how others will see them.

Suggestions
- Expose them to people who are risk takers and have them share their failures and successes
- Talk about the benefits and pitfalls of risks
- Teach them how to weigh their decisions
- Give them opportunities to step outside of their 'comfort zone' and try or experience new things
- Try new things together
- Remind them of other times in their lives when they have taken risks and it has paid off
- If you know they are interested in something but too shy to ask – tell a friend of theirs or call the school and let someone know

Be Patient

> "We boil at different degrees."
>
> — Clint Eastwood

70

This tip is much easier said than done. Showing patience isn't easy especially when they know all the right buttons to push. Tweens and teens require patience - lots and lots of patience. They are often looking to you to see how you react to and handle certain situations. They will make mistakes and they need you to demonstrate patience and understanding when they do.

Suggestions

- Try not to let your frustration show – when you do they either shut down or push you over the edge; either way isn't good
- To keep your temper and buy you time ask as many questions as you can and listen to the answers carefully
- Leave the room for a few minutes if you need some space, if they follow tell them you will give them the answer they don't want if they don't give you a few minutes
- Get on the phone with someone you can vent with, trust their advice, or who will distract you

Control anger

"I rant, therefore I am."

— Dennis Miller

71

Have you ever seen, heard of or experienced a situation where things improved because someone lost their temper? Controlling your anger, even when they have pushed you to the edge is important. They are watching your reactions and looking for direction.

Suggestions

- Avoid threatening or using threats that you can't follow through on (they will enjoy making you look foolish)
- Do not react out of anger – take time to think about why you are angry and what punishment would fit the crime
- Remember that their anger isn't always rational - teens will rant and rage and they need time to calm down too which might not be at your pace
- Find out what the problem is by asking them what they are angry about, and then ask them again in an hour – you might get a lot more details or a completely different answer
- Before speaking remember that when they are in a rage they hear nothing that you say, you are speaking to hear yourself – a complete waste of your time and energy

teach resilience

"He who is not courageous enough to take risks will accomplish nothing in life."

— Muhammad Ali

We all need a certain amount of resilience to survive in this world. Some people are born with it and some need to be taught it. Having resilience means that when life throws some curves or road blocks in your way you can overcome them and feel stronger because of it. Resilience is about being able to recover from change, illness, failures or misfortunes.

Suggestions
- For every negative thing your child can tell you about a situation find a positive
- Actively seek out solutions to problems rather than wasting time complaining about them
- Avoid "pity parties" where you let your child go on and on about what is wrong with their lives, without any plan to change what they can
- Teach your children how to look at a problem or situation from many different angles

Be Prepared

> "There cannot be a crisis next week. My schedule is already full."
>
> — Henry A. Kissinger

73

As you might already know, the disastrous events, life threatening emergencies or times when critical decisions need to be made often happen when one member of the family is absent or unavailable. Talking about or making some preparations for the 'what ifs' beforehand helps to alleviate some stress and can be a life saver.

Suggestions

- Have a list of emergency contacts on the fridge along with all the numbers needed to contact you
- Designate a person in your neighbourhood or close by that your kids could call upon or house they could go to if they are locked out or there is a problem with the house
- Go over your fire plan
- Have a list of reliable contractors that are on call 24hrs (plumber, electrician, etc.)
- Get CAA or AAA for your car(s) – you won't regret this investment and even if you never use it, your peace of mind is worth it
- Create a storage area or shelf in a pantry closet that is for emergency, long life, easy to prepare food items, a selection of batteries, flashlights, etc. (see Tip 16 for Emergency kit details)

Bullying

> *"Never be bullied into silence. Never allow yourself to be made a victim. Accept no one's definition of your life; define yourself."*
>
> — Harvey Fierstein

The reality is that most teens are either bullying or bullied at some point in their teenage years. Just because it is a reality doesn't mean that it should be accepted as something that they have to endure or a necessary part of growing up. Bullying can be extremely destructive and regardless of which end they are on, it is definitely something to talk about and stop.

Suggestions
- Contact the school, team, community centre, etc. to inform them of everything that you know and ask what steps will be taken
- Get a notebook and document incidences with dates, times and people involved
- Listen to your teen and ask why they think this is happening but keep an open mind and remember about there always being two sides to a story
- Get your child age appropriate books with characters that have experienced bullying so that they feel less isolated.
- Supervise your child's internet usage, email accounts and text messages as a lot of bullying occurs through these mediums

Choose your battles

> "Lose as if you like it; win as if you were used to it"
>
> — Tommy Hitchcock

75

Gaining control in your household means that you need to carefully choose what battles to go to war over and what ones to let go of. Like other wars there are sometimes winners, losers, and casualties. If you go to war on everything - big and little things will appear to be valued the same way. If you don't engage in any battles they will continue to try and find your limits and continually push the boundaries.

Suggestions

- As parents, make joint decisions and agreements and present a united front whenever possible
- Make sure you choose not only your battles but your battleground too - choosing to argue it out at the wrong time and in the wrong place can add to your problems
- Make sure you know what you are really battling about – a solution won't be found if you don't know what the real issues are
- Don't gloat if you are victorious and admit defeat gracefully if there has to be a winner at all.

Negotiations

"The first rule of holes: when you're in one, stop digging"
— Molly Ivins

76

Teens can try to hold you hostage when they want something; sometimes you have to negotiate, but avoid entering into win/lose negotiations. Provide as many options and solutions as possible. Do not fall for the 'wearing you down' technique, the relentless bombardment, or the 'all my friends' parents said yes' line. If you say 'yes' then it should be because it is what is best and right, and if you say 'no' it should be because it is unsafe or not in your child's best interests.

Suggestions

- Before entering into negotiations know what they want and what your bottom line is
- State your reasons clearly and once
- When you say 'no' mean it, so only use it when you have no intention of negotiating
- When negotiating you should not be the only one making concessions – make sure you are ending your negotiations in a win-win situation
- Only negotiate when calm and unrushed
- End all negotiations whenever voices get raised or threats are made
- Negotiations are not based on bribery
- All involved members should be present or involved in negotiations

"Life is change. Growth is optional. Choose wisely"

— John F. Kennedy

Moving 77

Moving schools or houses is a life shattering/changing event for teens. These moves can be extremely stressful for teens when much of their lives is about friends and familiarity. Making a move as smooth as possible for your teens is difficult but not impossible and it starts with your attitude. You cannot change the situation, only your attitude towards it. Help your teens accept the change by finding as many positive things about moving as you can.

Suggestions

- Get as much information as you can about your new community or school – things that are offered, special attractions, what it is close to, etc.
- Take tons of pictures of your new home, the area, the school(s), the town, local attractions and places of interest so that you can refer to them
- Go to your child's new school and ask them about registration, what documentation is needed, their website address, program information
- Even if you are dreading it, be honest but also share positive angles to change

Drugs & Alcohol

> "Drugs are a waste of time. They destroy your memory and your self-respect and everything that goes along with your self esteem."
>
> — Kurt Cobain

Alcohol is everywhere and there are drugs at every school and in every community. You may not be able to change that, but you can prepare and educate your children so that they can make informed decisions and choices. It is misguided to think there won't be opportunities for your children to try drugs or binge drink, but you can help them make it easier to say no.

Suggestions

- You should have a 'no matter what hour of the night policy'. Your teens should be able to call you no matter what time of the night
- NEVER get angry about the phone call as it will determine if you ever get another one
- It is your job to give your child excuses to give to their 'friends' or fellow party goers (ex: My parents told me that if I did any drugs tonight that I could kiss away the car usage, etc.)
- Do your research – Google official names and street names for drugs and learn about them, their effects, and warning signs
- Talk to your teens about drugs and alcohol (give them facts rather than opinions)

Daily physical, human contact is essential for growth. Your teens need to be hugged, even if it is not something you are comfortable with. They will seek out physical comfort and you don't want them seeking it out from other people. Make hugging your children part of your daily routine.

Suggestions

- Get over your own personal discomfort and put your teens needs first
- Tell your teen that you need a daily hug and give them the option of choosing when to do it
- Don't embarrass your teen by doing it at times or in places that would make them feel uncomfortable (ex. in front of friends or at school)
- Encourage them to initiate the hug or ask them for one and then you know they are in a place and time where it is a comfortable thing for them to do
- Even when they tell you they don't need one or push you away – they do; it might not be the right time or place at that moment, but make sure they get one that day

Make packages

> "Always have a vivid imagination, for you never know when you might need it"
>
> — *J.K. Rowling*

80

Teens love getting mail and getting a package of things that say "I know you and I love you" is another way to show them they are important. Making them a package for them to say good luck, hang in there, study survival package, etc. will make them feel understood and supported.

Suggestions
- Don't spend a lot of money on a package or survival kit.
- To make it more affordable, collect things every now again and keep them in a shoe box until the time is right
- Include pictures or notes to bring a smile to their faces or know you love them
- Make packages for studying, a break up, valentines, good luck at school, camp, etc.

Depression & Anxiety

> "Excellence is not a singular act but a habit. You are what you repeatedly do."
>
> — Shaquille O'Neal

81

A certain amount of anxiety or sadness is a normal and healthy part of teen life. If your teen has sustained periods of sadness or anxiety you should see your doctor as they may need professional support and/or counselling. Anxiety can be debilitating and if not treated can lead to your teen not being able to cope with everyday life.

Suggestions
- Be comfortable asking your health care professional and risk being wrong
- Talk to your child about how they are feeling – if they are persistently feeling hopeless and helpless seek out advice from your healthcare professional
- Teen angst doesn't stay for weeks on end, with no breaks
- Be worried when they spend an excessive amont of time obsessing over things they cannot change, fixating on issues or unable to communicate effectively with others
- Be honest with your teen about your concerns
- Ask friends or family to assist you in getting your child help and support

Annoyed Wall

> "Life is a shipwreck, but we must not forget to sing in the lifeboats"
>
> — Francois-Marie Arouet Voltaire

82

Get a chalk board, dry erase or bulletin board and label it the annoyed wall. Everyone can have the opportunity to write or draw pictures of things or situations that are annoying them. It should be a humorous way of venting so that family members know what is on each other's minds, not something that becomes a toxic place for people to be hurtful, cruel or negative.

Suggestions
- If you are going to change or erase it, take a picture then look back and have a laugh about it
- Put the board in the bathroom, kitchen, laundry room – somewhere your family spends time
- Go over rules for the board – not being hurtful or spiteful towards other people or not getting caught up in the negative aspects of the situation
- Remind your family about its purpose: to find humour in life's little annoyances
- Keep it light and take down anything that would be offensive or hurtful
- Make the rules like; no names of specific people

Message board

"The best thing one can do when it's raining is to let it rain"

— Henry Wadsworth Longfellow

83

This board should be the place in the house where the expectation is that everyone takes and leaves messages. It should be easy to use. If you have one of these boards you should never hear "I didn't think you would see the note" or "I didn't know where to leave you a note".

Suggestions
- Put it in the highest traffic area of the house and near a phone
- Everyone should be in the habit of checking the message board daily so that you aren't hunting them down to give them a message
- If they don't take proper messages from your friends threaten to do the same with theirs
- Make rules about voice messages – only the person the message is for should erase it, etc.
- Keep the message area well stocked so there are no excuses for why complete messages weren't taken
- Do not let a message board be used as an excuse for not communicating directly – if they can contact you directly, they should

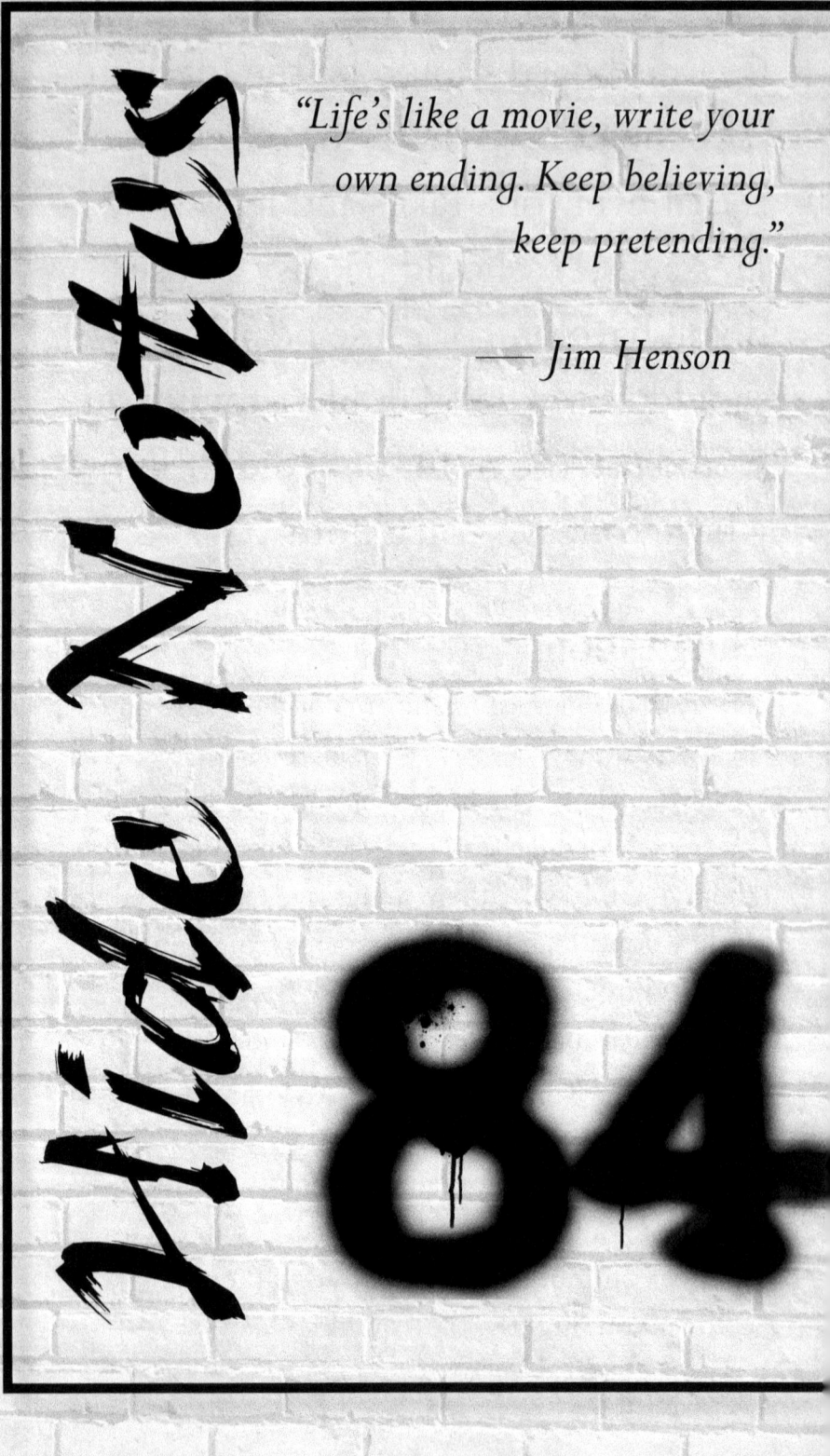

Putting notes in their drawers, bags, lunch, clothes, etc. is a great way to surprise them and give them a boost. It is another way of letting them know you care, are thinking of them and think of them often even when you may be 1000's of miles apart.

Suggestions
- Get a funky or colourful pad of paper - they will know as soon as they find one that it is from you
- Write positive sentiments, personal messages, jokes or quotes that will make them smile or laugh
- Make sure when you write notes, that they aren't embarrassing if someone else finds them
- Remember about seasonal things such as camping gear, winter clothes, coats, hats, suitcases, etc. as they will be places that notes can safely be hidden for months
- Create a whole pad of notes can be torn off and put in strategic places at strategic times
- Make sure some of your notes say important things that they need to hear from you regularly and in different ways
- www.sayplease.com has great notes to use too

contracts

"Food is the most primitive form of comfort"

— *Sheila Graham*

85

If you are somewhere and there is drinking then…, if you make a bad decision and need to call home then…, if you don't attend classes then…, if you stay out past your curfew the consequence will be…, etc. All tweens and teens have areas they could improve upon, as do parents. Contracts are for areas that never seem to improve even with a few stern discussions or consequences. Contracts help to provide further "incentives" to improve or change particular behaviours.

Suggestions

- If you make a contract it needs to be in writing and signed
- Contracts should be bound by dates and times
- All parties should be involved in making the contract
- The contract should be accessible to everyone involved so that you can remind yourself of its boundaries and expectations
- Make sure you have good incentives for keeping to the contract rather than just punishments for not keeping to it
- Make a copy of the contract in case it gets 'lost'

compliment

> "I make it a rule always to believe compliments implicitly for five minutes, and to simmer gently for twenty more."
>
> — Alice James

86

Make a mental note to compliment your teen(s) everyday. They need to hear the good things about themselves and their actions even if they roll their eyes at you or tell you that 'you have to say it because you are their parent'. Compliments should be genuine and well thought out so that they will be acknowledged and hopefully believed.

Suggestions

- Teach your children how to accept a compliment
- Don't allow your teens to belittle compliments or find a reason to refute them
- If you don't think they believe that particular compliment then say it again in the near future in a different way and give them another example of why you believe that
- Encourage the rest of your family to compliment each other – one meal a week each person has to think of compliments to tell each other
- Compliment yourself in front of others to give them ideas of things to say
- Don't say it if you don't mean it

Create a calendar

"Strength comes from waiting"

— *Jose Marti*

87

Family calendars keep you all sane and organized. All commitments, obligations, appointments, etc. should be kept on a calendar that is centrally located and easy to access. This keeps all family members 'in the know' and hopefully on schedule, on time, and up to date with family events and activities.

Suggestions

- Your teens will tell you that they will remember it – they won't – put it on a calendar
- Keep the calendar in a central location, near a pencil and in a high traffic area
- If you have a lot of children, colour code each child so their commitments are easy to distinguish from each other
- Buy a calendar with big squares so that you can write as much as you need to
- Make the calendar appealing to the eye or with funny sayings or jokes that will get your children to actually look at it

"Pain is temporary. It may last a minute, or an hour, or a day, or a year, but eventually it will subside and something else will take its place. If I quit, however, it lasts forever"

— Lance Armstrong

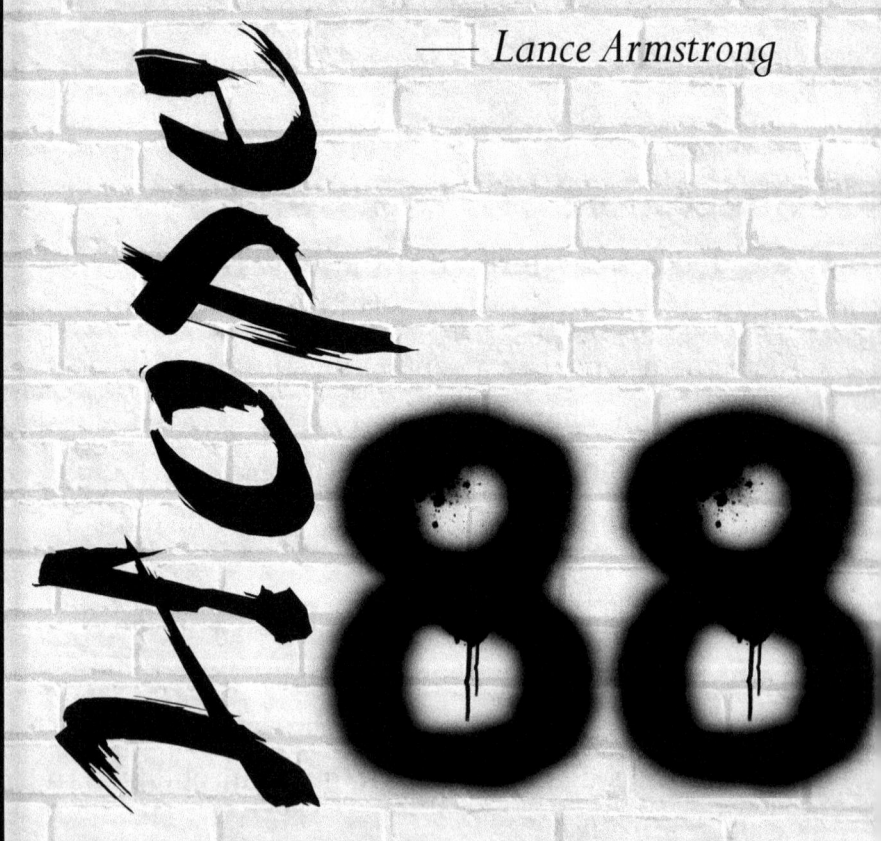

Having a sense of hope is essential. Your teens need you to have a sense of hope when they feel hopeless. Don't ever tell your teen that they or a situation is hopeless. They need you to give them a sense of hope even in situations that may appear hopeless. Dig deep and find something positive or inspiring to keep them hopeful without being dishonest. There is nothing wrong with saying a situation looks tough but there should always be a shred of hope for them to cling to if they need it.

Suggestions
- Never say never
- Teach your child the art of finding hope in what appears to be the most hopeless situations
- Never let them quit a situation, team, or activity because they think it is hopeless
- Demonstrate being tenacious and persistent by not giving up on your own obstacles, dreams and goals
- Help them to identify the difference between quitting and knowing when to cut your losses
- List things regularly that give you hope and offer them suggestions of things that make them hopeful

Whether you believe in pre-marital sex, think they should wait until they're 40 years old or support their right to chose when the time is right, you need to talk about sex and its consequences. Being open and honest with as little judgement as possible will encourage questions and knowledge that will help them with their decision making. If they aren't asking you, they may ask someone who has a vested interest and not an unbiased response!

Suggestions
- Bring it up, say the word (sex)
- Talk about signs that it is right or not right
- Talk about the importance of being clear with your intentions and your limits
- Have them live by the rule – "If you can't talk about it with each other, you aren't ready"
- If at all possible have them spend 24 hours with a newborn or very young baby (try finding a friend with a baby that has colic)
- Talk about sex and alcohol and impaired judgement and reduced inhibitions
- Even if you don't agree, talk about contraception – choices, options, effectiveness, abstinence, etc.

Tweens and teens need tons of sleep. This isn't because they are lazy but more because their brains and bodies are changing and developing. However, teens do need some direction and limits with sleep and their sleep patterns. Help them to keep their body clock set to the daytime and teach them good techniques to unwind at the end of the day before going to bed.

Suggestions
- Get them into a night time routine
- Use white noise (fan, window open, steady traffic, etc.) to relax them
- Do not use the TV or radio as a method of getting them to sleep – it stimulates their brain
- Try to avoid all nighters on the weekends as they mess up their internal clocks for the rest of the week
- Set bedtimes (yes, I said it) and stick to them (even if it is 1am)
- Computers and cell phones should be out of their rooms by a certain time or at the least insist that they are turned off and check that it is being followed

No Questions Asked

> "Life is a crisis – so what!"
>
> — *Malcolm Bradbury*

91

Make a rule in your house that your teen can call you for help with no questions asked AT THAT PARTICULAR TIME. You will not discuss it immediately but with the understanding a discussion will take place in the immediate future. They need to know that you will help them without making a scene, embarrassing them or making it worse. If they don't call you, they could get themselves into an even more unsafe situation or trouble.

Suggestions

- Talk about your policy well before you think you need to
- Emphasize that you will be talking about what happened, just not that night
- Make sure there are consequences, but there also needs to be some reward for doing the right thing and calling you
- Talk about strategies for next time – there will be a next time
- Do not get angry as they will shut down and you will accomplish nothing
- Avoid sighing, eye rolling, angry silences in the car on the way home
- Do not send another sibling instead. You don't know the whole story or have the full picture about the situation you are putting them in

> "Why is there so much month left at the end of money?"
>
> — *John Barrymore*

Money

92

If you can afford it, pay for certain extra chores or errands. Nothing talks like money to your teen. Sometimes it isn't worth your time to argue about it. Don't do it so often that it is expected but often enough to motivate them. Your kids should do things around the house because they are a part of your family but pay them for the responsibilities they take on.

Suggestions
- Do not pay for things that they should be doing anyway
- Make sure you have money in your household budget to do it
- Don't say you are going to pay them and then not follow through – getting them to do the next task will be next to impossible
- If you are paying make sure you get the quality of work you want – this teaches them about the world of work, expectations and taking pride in what they do
- When they ask if they are getting paid for a task always say yes (ex: "Yes, I am paying you in groceries, internet bill, cell phone bill, etc.)

Girlfriends/Boyfriends

> "Even though your kids will consistently do the exact opposite of what you're telling them to do, you have to keep loving them just as much."
>
> — Bill Cosby

Love or despise them, your teen's girlfriend or boyfriend needs to be accepted and made to feel welcome. Anything less, on your part, and you will alienate your child. This isn't to say you can't give an opinion but you need to keep them as factual as possible and brief. Your opinion isn't really wanted and giving it too aggressively will only put them further into the arms of their boyfriend or girlfriend.

Suggestions

- Do not question their judgement - when you question their choices you are telling them you don't trust them to make good decisions
- For every negative thing you say about their boyfriend or girlfriend find two positive things
- Make your home the place they want to be
- Talk to your teen about what they want and need from their relationship
- Share your dating disaster stories and other such nightmares
- Talk to your teens about the different types of love you can feel for different people
- They will make mistakes. Be supportive and non-judgemental so it will be you that they turn to when it all goes wrong

countdown

> "Once you have mastered time, you will understand how true it is that most people overestimate what they can accomplish in a year - and underestimate what they can achieve in a decade!"
>
> — Tony Robbins

94

Teens are often so absorbed in their own lives (particularly social lives) that they are not always realistic with time and timelines. Keep very visual countdowns going in your house for important things like days until the end of school, until exams, etc. Be creative about how you count or mark days passed so that they can get a better sense of and be more realistic about their future.

Suggestions

- Money jar – put an amount of money in (ex. $1/day) for every day they are at school, spend it on something really fun in the summer
- Candy Jar – put enough candies in the jar so that each day someone in your family can eat one, when the jar is empty it is exam time
- Knotted rope – tie knots in a rope that equal the number of days until something and then each day they can untie one
- Buy a chalkboard for the kitchen or bathroom and mark off another day that has passed that you are closer to a goal or event
- If you are planning a holiday, give your family a clue-a-day about where you are going, for how long, and when

Exceptionalities 95

> "What's important is finding out what works for you"
>
> — *Henry Moore*

All children are exceptional but some learn differently and need additional help and/or support. This can be draining on a family. If your child needs additional support at school or accessing programs in the community, you are their strongest and sometimes only advocate.

Suggestions

- Look up what agencies are located near you that service your needs
- Keep documentation about their educational requirements for the school. Never hand over originals unless you have to and only after they have made a copy for you to keep
- Keep a record of people that you speak to and contact numbers with a note about what you talked about
- When changing schools, speak with the school staff to give them as much information as possible and create the best possible start for your child
- As your child gets older, include them in the process so that they will learn how to properly and appropriately advocate for themselves

Re-decorate

> "I'm not a sponge exactly, but I find that something I look at is a great opportunity for ideas."
>
> — *Martha Stewart*

96

Teens need changes that they can control. If they want to re-decorate their room, let them. If you are invited to be a part of it, jump at the chance to spend time with your child. Re-decorating doesn't have to be expensive but it is a good chance to clean up or out a room and change the daily scenery.

Suggestions

- Go to a thrift store or discount department store and let them choose some new accessories for their room
- Re-paint the room
- Move the furniture around
- Do a huge clear out of anything that hasn't been used in the last two years
- Look at garage sales or inexpensive furniture stores for new or gently used furniture
- Go on-line or look through magazines for ideas
- Be involved as much or as little as they ask you
- Give them a budget to work with themselves – this will be a very simple and quick lesson of how far money can go and not go

Critical Information

> "All life is an experiment.
> The more experiments you
> make the better."
>
> — Ralph Waldo Emerson

97

Get a book or complete an information sheet that contains essential information about the house, finances, contacts, travel documentation, wills, extra keys, mortgage, bill payments, family numbers and information, etc. There should also be an information sheet with phone numbers, email addresses, etc.

Suggestions

- Find a neighbour you trust and give them names and phone numbers of people to contact if particular emergencies occur
- Give your teens a copy of the critical contact information, location of fuse box, alarm company number, water shut off location, etc.
- Make a house manual
- Have a safe place to store all original documents and do not allow them to store their own
- Share information about your will – they need to know what your wishes and intentions are so that should the worst happen there are no surprises

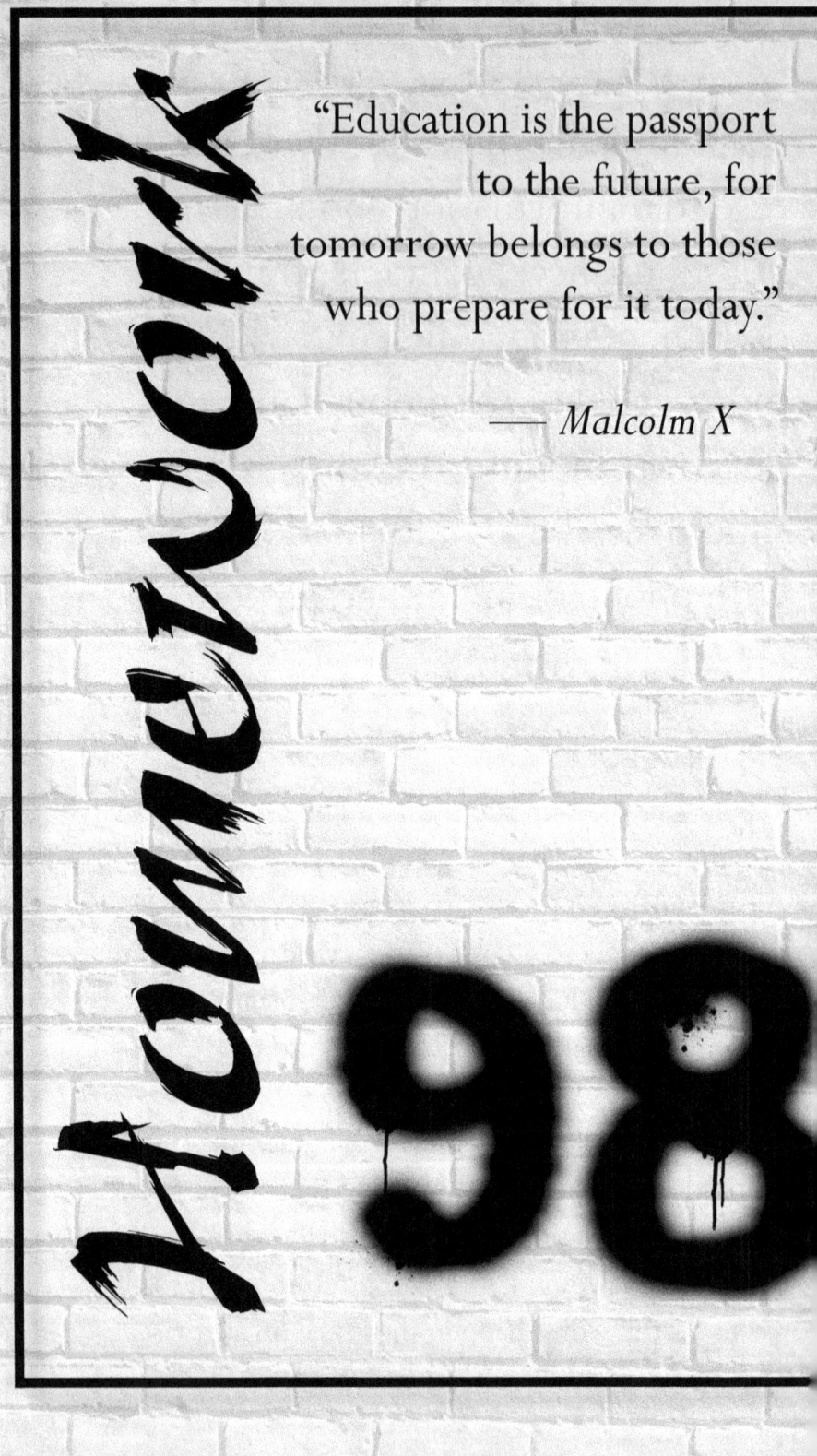

Ideally your child should have no more than 5 – 10 minutes of homework per grade they are in (ex: to a maximum of 90 mins in high school). Your child should think of school much like a job, if they work hard all day there should be little to do in the evening. If your child is experiencing an overwhelming amount of homework contact the school to find out why this might be the case.

Suggestions

- Set a particular time to do homework in your house
- Have a quiet area where work can get done
- Ensure that homework is getting done when they are on the computer and they are not instant messaging with friends or pointlessly surfing the internet
- If homework is not being completed, have consequences ready (no sports, no internet, etc.)
- Some schools are using the internet to post assignments; if your child's school does this, go on and see what they have due
- Get the email addresses of their teachers and check in regularly to make sure your children are staying on track

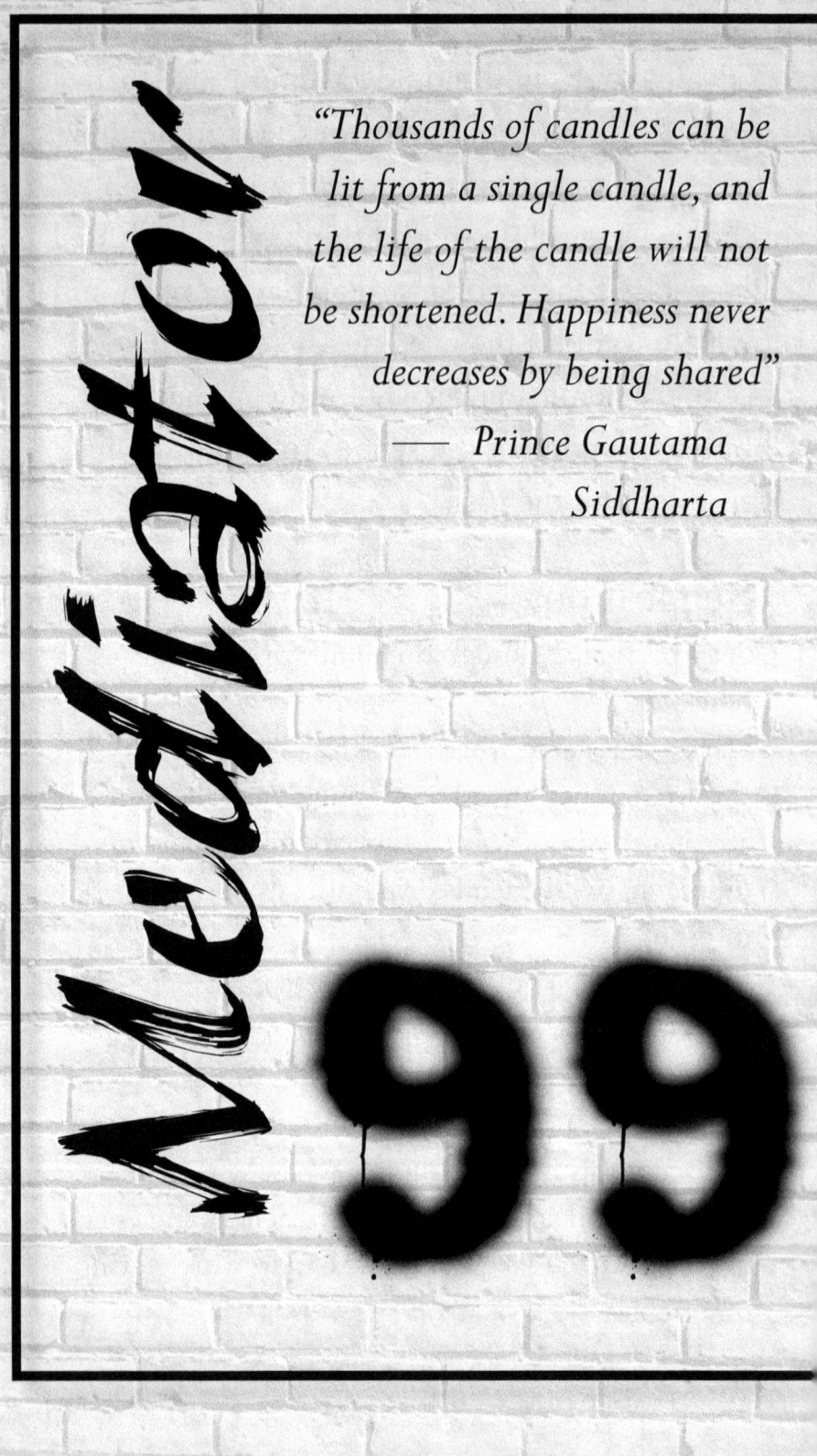

Get someone who can be your mediator/'go-between'/family friend who is 'cool' (unlike their parents). It is a tall order; make sure that you choose wisely. You need someone who your children trust but also consider fun, honest, loving and wise. They will be the person your tween or teen should feel they can call when they believe you wouldn't understand, 'get it' or would 'freak out'. This person should be your back up and your support.

Suggestions

- A mediator should be a good listener and give advice sparingly
- Make sure your mediator is 100% trustworthy
- Use this person only in situations that you cannot see any resolution or in emergency situations where you need them to listen immediately
- Ask the person before you give them this role; if they don't like being in the position they are definitely not going to be good with it
- Make sure your mediator or 'go-between' has all of your contact information at any given time
- Include them as a contact at the school, with your family member's unit or on documentation where it gives you this option

Best On The Block

> "I think I've discovered the secret of life - you just hang around until you get used to it."
>
> — Charles M. Schulz

100

Make your house the place friends like coming to. It will be important to make sure that you know as much as possible about each friend choice and the best way to do this is get to know them. Just remember that this doesn't mean you have to let them drink, smoke or let go of all house rules but it should be a place where people are welcomed, mutually respected and can have fun.

Suggestions
- Pay for pizza or take out – food continues to be something they will come home and stay home for
- Have an area in the house that is considered theirs with the understanding that you will be coming by/through/in and out of/into whenever the mood strikes you
- Depending on your budget and child's interests spend some money on some gadgets, gaming system, pool, pool table, sports equipment, etc. It will be a lot cheaper than a permanent record or a lawyer for something foolish they did because they were bored or unsupervised
- Do regular check-ins – dropping off laundry in their room or offering up some dessert
- Remember your sense of humour with their friends and pick your battles

Read this book together!

"Realize that the journey and the goal are always the same"
—— Dr. Wayne W. Dyer

101

Read this book with your spouse, best friend, partner, loved one. Being a parent is a tough job at times. We hope you find some words of wisdom, laughter, and support in this book.

For more information about our books, resources, or tips visit our website at: www.wywa.org

To submit a tip of your own, write to: Megan@whileyouwereaway.org

Notes:

www.ingramcontent.com/pod-product-compliance
Lightning Source LLC
LaVergne TN
LVHW051553070426
835507LV00021B/2558